COMBOS
FOR YOUTH GROUPS
VOL. 2

6 MONTH-LONG THEMES WITH THE WORKS

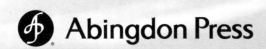

Abingdon Press

MANUFACTURED IN THE UNITED STATES OF AMERICA

Anne Broyles, writer of Road Trip, is an ordained clergywoman and curriculum writer. She has written also for COMBOS, Volume 1, and for *Synago.* Anne lives in Malibu, California.

Sam Halverson, who wrote Who Do You Say? and God Loves Good Sex, is ordained clergy, serving at First United Methodist Church in Lancaster, Ohio. He is the author of *Destination Unknown: 50 Mystery Trips.*

Barb McCreight created Picture This! She says her creativity comes from long experience as a teacher of young children, but she currently finds joy in serving as youth director at First United Methodist Church in Bryant, Arkansas.

David Stewart contributed Beyond Belief and much of the introductory information to this volume. He is a key person in the development of COMBOS and has brought to the resource the richness of his experience in youth ministry in Georgia and Tennessee.

Crys Zinkiewicz pulled together Rescue 911. She is the senior editor of youth resources for The United Methodist Publishing House and lives in Nashville, Tennessee.

05 06 07 08 09 10 11 12 13 14—10 9 8 7 6 5 4 3 2 1

contents

Basic Menu

Games

Build relationships as you have fun!

Share and Care Groups

Care for one another; experience a loving community; start to think about the topic.

Focus Point

Use a visual or dramatic way to start the thinking.

Focus Thoughts

Connect the Christian faith to the lives of your youth.

Focus Group

Give students a way to process what they've heard and done.

Closing

Provide reflection and commitment time.

Fixin's

Munchies

Serve food with a message!

Popular Music

Capture the attention of the youth.

Worship & Praise Music

Make God Smile!

Other Movie Options

Use these instead of the recommended video for Focus Point, if you choose.

Create-a-Video Ideas

Put your students to work on the theme!

On-the-Street Interviews

Get opinions from others to jump start the group.

Instead of a Message

Try a book or a panel.

Out and About Ideas

Go off-site for insight!

Service Project Ideas

Put faith into action.

Announcement Ideas

Add zest to the rest.

Special

Add an unforgettable event or service.

More Closing Ideas

Choose from suggested rituals, readings, and remembrances to remind your youth of God's love for them!

Leader Helps

Leader Scripture Exploration

Learn from additional Bible passages related to the theme.

Talk Tips

Add a touch to make the talk livelier and more engaging.

PUBLICITY & DECORATIONS

Appetizers

Choose from these great ideas to publicize the theme—not only to your group members but also to their friends and the community. You're inviting youth to come to Christ!

Spice It Up!

Create an inviting atmosphere. Crank up the fun! Let the walls and the space shout your message!

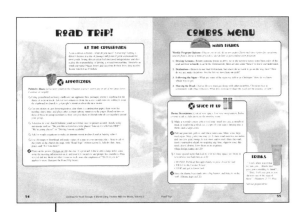

CD-ROM STUFF

Recipes

Create food that is good, fun, and says something about the theme.

Additional Games

Choose a different game if none of the others suit you.

Additional Questions

Take the conversation in a different direction if that's what your group needs.

Handouts

Give students the tools they need.

How-to Instructions

Provide the information needed to make a burning bush or do a witness statement, for example.

Focus Thoughts

Start with the text of the printed version to prepare your own talk for your own youth. Add your personal stories; put the message in the context of your youth group and community.

Theme Logos

Use the art to build your publicity flyers, t-shirts, and decorations.

On Screen Presentations

Go high-tech and big screen! Reinforce your words with powerful images.

Posters

Send home or hang up cool posters.

Scripts

Print out the scripts to the skits so your youth can easily present them.

Youth Witness Statements

Read these for inspiration and for an example of a witness statement.

Worship Helps

Use these ready-to-go worship ideas, guided meditations, litanies, and other helps.

THEMES—
LESS WORK! MORE IMPACT!

COMBOS is theme-based programming. Why use themes? There are benefits for you and your group!

Themes help you be prepared each week. Creating a weekly program can be a daunting task even for the most accomplished of speakers and program developers. When you use a theme, such as "Rescue 9-1-1," you create a road map to guide your thinking and increase your impact. You can begin putting together songs, games, video clips, food, needed volunteers, and publicity weeks in advance. You can even assign jobs to key volunteers and youth leaders.

Themes also keep you from focusing on the same topics over and over (which gives youth permission to drop out).

Themes provide week-to-week connection but do not require week-to-week attendance for youth in two-house families.

Themes make it easier to advertise. Publicity helps parents know what is going on. It also helps students know when to invite their friends and when topics might not be appropriate for their friend's first visit.

Themes help you develop ideas that will appeal to your current youth participants and help your church reach out to new youth.

Themes allow youth to have fun while, at the same time, exploring serious life and faith issues. The programs deal with topics relevant to youth, such as dating, being authentic, placing God first, making and keeping friends, and persevering through hard times. The programs focus on being a Christian, making decisions as a Christian, and discovering God's purposes for life. The messages, small group time, discussion, worship, and service projects are specifically designed to help students grow in their faith.

Themes generate more creativity. Since you know what programs are coming up, you will be more apt to think about things that relate to the topic—and have time to pull them off. Feel free to add ideas of your own. These programs are guidelines for your use. Omit or change anything that doesn't fit your particular setting. Use every tool at your disposal to spread the Word.

YES, BUT WE DON'T HAVE...

The Numbers

If you have fewer than ten teens, COMBOS might not be for you. Instead, check out *Single-Digit Youth Groups: Working With Fewer Than 10 Teens* (Abingdon Press). However, you don't have to have a hundred or even twenty youth to put together a dynamic Combo! Share and Care or Focus Groups can be as few as three or four. Instead of six teams for a game, two teams are just fine. You don't have to do a stand-up "talk"; sit down together and do a discussion around the points you would have made. COMBOS is highly adaptable.

The Space

Does the image of a full-sized gymnasium cast a pall on your enthusiasm? That size room is not essential; you may need to be creative with the space you have, but you can fix a Combo that will fit. Consider using the sanctuary for the Focus Point, Focus Thoughts, Focus Group, and Closing. Share and Care Groups can meet in corners of larger rooms or in multiple smaller rooms. Adapt games for smaller spaces, or play outside.

The Equipment

You certainly may use projection equipment, but you do not have to. Youth groups of all sizes have managed without VCRs or PowerPoint® for years. Choose other options or use printed sheets, instead of projected words. Have students look in Bibles, instead of on screen. Teach a new song by singing one line at a time and having the youth repeat the line, then singing the song several times. You can do it! (Just think, you don't have to worry about the equipment not working!)

The Adult Leaders

One thing about COMBOS is that adult volunteers don't have to feel that they must "do it all" or be "the expert." Having the pieces of the Combo identified means that you can ask *specific people*—adults and youth—for *specific help,* which is more easily given. One person can fix food; another lead games. For more on leaders, see page 9.

SHARE AND CARE GROUPS VS. FOCUS GROUPS

Both "Share and Care Groups" and "Focus Groups" are used in COMBOS. Do you need both? That's up to you. Here are descriptions of what they are intended to do. You get to put together whatever works best for you.

Share and Care Groups: Checking In

Student ministry focuses on Jesus' commandment to "love one another" as the heart of our faith. Share and Care Groups (or whatever you decide to call them) teach students how to love. Something about opening our lives to one another puts us in the presence of God. Many sharing experiences are from the most intimate moments of life—truly, a path to holy ground.

In a Share and Care Group, students are able to talk openly about what is going on in their lives—their joys and their struggles (highs and lows of the week). These groups provide safe spaces and people who really listen to and support one another. Group members become very close. They develop the *koinonia,* or fellowship, that the New Testament speaks of and students long for.

To achieve that level of intimacy, consider these guidelines:

• Have the same persons in the same group each week.
• Keep the group small (four to seven persons).
• Group by same gender.
• Stress consistent attendance; ask that students let someone in the group know if they must be absent. It takes time to develop a community of friends who trust one another and care deeply about each other.
• Work with your leaders so that they grow in their group leadership skills.

When Share and Care Groups meet, the student or adult leader for the particular group begins the time with prayer. Then each group member tells a high and a low for the past week. Or if time is limited, the leader may ask whether anyone had anything really good or bad happen during the past week. Individuals with serious issues may ask the leader for time to tell a personal concern prior to or after the meeting. Groups end the "checking-in" time with prayer requests and prayer led by a student.

An adult or a mature youth can be a group leader, responsible for the well-being of his or her group. The leader

• Reminds group members to listen carefully with their ears and hearts, focusing on the person who is speaking and being careful not to interrupt.
• Helps group members understand one another's feelings and learn to love God, others, and themselves.
• Does not allow group members to talk about persons who are not present. This is not a gossip session.
• Allocates time so that all persons have a chance to talk.
• Encourages members to pray daily for the group.

Leaders may also have activities outside of the regular meeting time, keep in touch during the week by e-mail or phone, and send birthday cards to group members.

A Share and Care Group is literally a laboratory for life. What is learned is used over and over outside the group. Learning how to heal one broken relationship helps an individual work on other relationships. Learning how to weather one crisis helps an individual face the next.

Share and Care Groups: Warm Up

Depending on the time, Share and Care Groups can also start the youth thinking about the topic. Within the safety of the group, the youth can begin talking about their perspectives and experiences related to the topic. COMBOS provides questions, but you may choose to select others from the Focus Group list, from the extra ones on the CD-ROM, or ones that you create yourself.

Focus Groups: Study and Discussion

In contrast to the Share and Care Groups, Focus Groups function more for the moment. The "group" is formed at the time; it does not have the continuity of a Share and Care Group. Focus Group time is for debriefing the message, for taking it further, for personalizing its impact. The assignment for the group may be Bible study, discussion, or a specific activity.

Check the CD-ROM for additional questions that you may use for either Share and Care Warm Up or for Focus Groups; or feel free to create new questions or activities of your own.

MUSIC AND WORSHIP

COMBOS *gives you two types of music suggestions: popular songs and worship and praise music. Draw from the lists ones that appeal to you and your group; feel free to add other favorites.*

Popular Songs

Play these during welcoming, transitions, or exiting times. Having popular songs as part of the youth group experience engages youth, especially those who do not attend regularly. For some students, hearing popular songs dispels some negative preconceived notions about "church."

Worship and Praise Music

Music is important to youth—not just what they listen to on radios or their CD players. Music as an integral part of worship speaks to hearts and gives voice to faith.

Depending on your schedule, you may want to have more than one time of worship and praise music.

Consider creating a band of your own. (Information on CD)

Worship: Create Space for God to Work

Worship points people to God. It is not a feeling or formula. Focus energy on a single point and keep it simple.

Remind youth leaders that they are lead worshippers not performers (this is a challenge for many youth). Help them be prepared. ALWAYS offer encouragement. Hold your leaders accountable for personal growth and private worship.

After each worship, ask: Did God smile?

How to Involve Parents

Parents are some of your best resources for youth group. Try some of these ideas to use their expertise and their energy and to make things easier on you. They may thank you for the opportunity to be with their child.

- Ask parents to handle details such as taking attendance; setting up games, snacks, and the worship center; and especially welcoming the youth.

- Let parents do the driving. They're already used to chauffeuring; so on that next out and about or service project, why not put them to work? It's a no-brainer way to make them feel needed, which they are!

- Invite parents to serve on a panel for a topic. Recruit parents who are willing to talk openly about their lives, but talk in advance with them about the topic and some questions that may arise. Establish rules for the session to protect the participants. (A good rule of thumb is that any parent can opt out of any question if desired.)

- Ask parents to secretly write a letter to their youth, telling about something in their life as it relates to the topic you choose (for example, a time when the parent experienced God's grace or the forgiveness of someone). During worship time, hand out the letters to the youth. Let them go to a private corner to read the letters alone. For some parents, this letter is an ideal way to share important information; the experience can spawn some serious parent-kid talk. (Note: You need to be ready to write letters to those young people whose parents do not take the time or the effort to do this.)

—Barb McCreight

Leadership

Using **COMBOS** *gives you a great vehicle for involving various people in leadership—adults and youth. You can ask them to do discreet tasks as well as work as a leadership team—two great ways to develop leadership!*

Plan

Start with the youth. Gather your student leaders, and ask them to look over the Combos. Talk about how to customize each program. (Having the student leaders meet first will show you what really appeals to youth.)

Add your adult leaders. Have a student present the plans and then allow the total team of student leaders and adults to come up with more ideas. (Some adults may be taken aback by being left out of the initial planning session. Help them see that it is important that you hear from the youth in an uninhibited situation. Let them know that adults do play an important role. You are not shutting them out or rejecting their skills.)

Map out two to three months. Have your student and adult leaders develop a strategy to carry out the plans. Divide the team into work groups (games, worship, service, food, publicity). If a work group needs more help or expertise, they may invite/draft other adults or students for the specific task. (And when persons feel successful at one task, they are more willing to serve in other ways.)

Go for it! Advertise in every way you can. Some ideas are included in this book for you to use as a springboard. Encourage your group to come up with more ideas. Order some t-shirts. (You may want to give your leaders a complimentary t-shirt for all their hard work.) Decorate your space. And have a blast!

Lead by Example

Here is a sampling of specific tasks that adult and student leaders can perform weekly:

Before the Program Begins
- Greet students.
- Help with student sign in.
- Look for visitors and help connect them with other students.

- Help in the kitchen with food and drinks.
- Set up for games.
- Cue up anything to be projected.

During Games, Program, Worship
- Help communicate game rules and objectives.
- Spread out across the room during the program time.
- Remember to be first to clap and sing.
- Without causing a scene, encourage students to be quiet and listen.
- Help keep Focus Groups on task.

After the Main Session
- Say goodbye to as many students as possible.
- Help clean up.

Share and Care Group Leaders
- During the week, write or call students who were absent from your small group.
- Pray for your group members.

Up-Front Leadership Opportunities

Here are some ways to involve students in leadership and to develop their leadership skills:

- Making announcements—The task is to communicate, but to do so in a way that is fun and memorable.

- Giving a witness statement—See the CD-ROM for help in preparing a testimony.

- Explaining a game, leading the singing, reading Scripture, leading a closing ritual.

Behind the Scenes

All adult and student leaders are expected to commit to their own spiritual growth through regular participation in congregational worship, prayer, Bible study, and other spiritual disciplines.

Leaders who are strong in their faith and faith practices will set the tone for others and undergird the ministry as a whole.

Sample Schedules

COMBOS *are meant to fit your timeframe. The larger the group you have to manage, the more tightly you will want to adhere to a planned schedule. Here are some sample schedules, including a "cue sheet."*

Sample Two-Hour Block
6:00   Games and Food
6:25   Share and Care Groups
6:50   Program (Focus Point, Focus Thoughts, Focus Group)
7:50   Worship
8:00   End

Sample One-Hour Block, especially for Middle School
6:00   Food and Games
6:25   Program (Focus Point, Focus Thoughts, Focus Group—Abbreviated)
6:55   Worship
7:00   End

Sample One-and-One-Half-Hour Block
6:00   Share and Care Groups
6:25   Program (Focus Point, Focus Thoughts, Focus Group—Abbreviated)
7:10   Worship
7:20   Food and Socializing
7:30   End

Sample Program and Cue Sheet
5:30   Welcome/Sign In/Nametags

5:40   Food and Games

6:00   Countdown Video or PowerPoint®

6:05   Band Jam/Popular Song (Throw out t-shirts to get youth excited or have a drawing for a cool prize.)

6:08   Opening Celebration (2–3 fast worship songs by the band or taped with words on screen)

6:18   Welcome and announcements (guy and girl co-hosts, written in advance); make this time funny as well as informative.

6:22   Program Introduction (Speaker)/Student Prayer

6:25   Focus Point Skit, Activity, or Video Clip

6:30   Scripture/Message by Speaker

6:50   Small Groups (in the meeting room to avoid moving from room to room)

7:20   Student Participation (witness statement, solo, dance, art on PowerPoint, poem…)

7:25   Worship (2–3 slow songs, 3 fast songs)

7:50   Closing/Sending Forth

8:00   End

10 Tips for Playing Games

1. Use games to attract new teens, to help them connect with others, and to ensure they'll want to come back!

2. Be prepared. Have all the supplies ready to go.

3. Use existing groups (small groups, grade groups, gender groups) to avoid wasting time creating teams.

4. Give instructions clearly and quickly. Keep them simple. Go over activities with leaders in advance.

5. Be excited! Remind your adult and student leaders that they set the tone for others to follow.

6. Remind adults they are to play too. They are not the group police. They are relationship builders.

7. As the leader, look for chances to play! This allows students to see a different side of you.

8. Avoid games that waste food. (People are hungry.)

9. Never force a student to play. Allow for spectators.

10. If a game goes bad (and they do!), laugh and simply enjoy your group members.

THE TALK

COMBOS gives you a section called Focus Thoughts. Although occasionally this time may vary in format, for the most part these are talks, or the "message." Whether or not you use the talk, be sure to read it because it ties together all the pieces of the theme.

Master Teacher

Focus Thoughts is your opportunity to share yourself, your thoughts, your dreams, your vision, and God's word. You can become the master teacher for your group. Don't be shy! Try it!

On the CD-ROM is the text or outline of the printed message. Use it as a beginning point for developing your own talk. Work with the text to customize it. To be effective in this medium, you really need to adapt the content to fit who you are and who your students are. Add personal stories of your own and references to your own group's experiences that will make it come alive for your particular youth.

Be sure that you, as a youth leader, have earned the right to be heard before you try to take your group into deep waters, dealing with touchy teen subjects. If your youth know that you care about them, you can say some things in a very direct way.

Talk Tips

Do a Scripture search and study of your own when preparing your particular talk, even if you use what is given here as the base. Start with the Focus Scripture, then expand to the Leader Exploration Scriptures given in the margin. Decide what will be the heart of your message. God may lead you in a different direction, more toward what your students need.

Tell personal stories. These make you more real and approachable, as well as give students concrete examples of what you mean.

Have the students talk about a question you ask. You can do this within the talk, "Nudge your neighbor" is an easy way to engage students with one another as well as with the topic. You may also ask students to "fill in the blank" verbally as you leave open some element and ask them to supply the information. Try asking them to repeat something you have just said. These techniques make the talk more interactive and less like a sermon.

Read the Bible. If you have projection equipment, you may want to read the Scripture passage from the screen, which makes it appear as though you are part of the audience. Or read from your Bible and have students read along with what is projected. Another way to do the Scripture readings is to have student volunteers read. Be sure that they can be heard. (You may want to do some coaching on reading well in public.) Explain the passage in your own words. What is the main point (not three—just one). Never assume knowledge, especially Bible knowledge!

Write down your outline and use it when you speak. Your students will appreciate that you spent some time working on your talk—not just flying by the seat of your pants.

Have a time of reflection, and ask the group to close their eyes and think about a question you ask. Come up with a challenge for the week. Give instructions for small group discussions.

Use a video camera to record yourself so that you can learn how to improve your verbal and non-verbal communication skills.

Print each week's message in a brochure. Yes, a brochure! Giving out a printed copy will allow students and adults a chance to read what you have already said (good reinforcement!). They can also take the brochure and share it with their friends and family. Your message will become seeds for so many who might never come to hear you speak.

WHO DO YOU SAY?

SAY IT WITH CERTAINTY

Son of God, prophet, teacher, King of kings, God incarnate, Savior of the world—there are so many titles for Jesus. What do they all mean? And have you allowed yourself to be introduced to who Jesus really is? The disciples, Jesus' closest friends, were asked who they said Jesus was; and only Peter could answer, "You are the Christ." What does that mean? Who do you say that Jesus is? Why?

APPETIZERS (Resources on CD)

Publicity Ideas: *As Christians we are called to be "fishers of people." Simply getting a non-believing youth into the church is a huge step. Don't neglect advertising (within your church and elsewhere). God works in miraculous ways—sometimes through very small and inexpensive things. Select any or all of the ideas below. Combine or simplify. Use your imagination. Invite a team of youth to decide how to personalize each program. Create a timeline for maximum effect. Spread the word with passion.*

- Post the posters. Use the <u>poster</u> or the <u>theme logo</u> (<u>Design on CD</u>); add times, dates, and locations. Post them wherever youth will be.

- Print and send postcards (<u>Design on CD</u>). Give additional postcards to group members to mail to friends.

- Ask questions about who Jesus is weeks before the program begins during announcement times, before outings—anytime the youth get together. When they give an answer, ask a hypothetical question around that statement. For example: If an answer is, "He's God's son." Ask: Does that mean Jesus and God are two different beings and we worship more than one being? Be careful not to get into a discussion right there. Just point out that these kinds of questions and more will be covered at this upcoming series.

- If you choose to videotape random on-the-street interviews, make sure that you have cards to hand out that read something like this: Want to see yourself onscreen? Come to (*insert where and the date and time*). Present this card for a free (*insert the item or service your group will give the bearer*).

- Have the youth fill out the questionnaire (<u>Handout on CD</u>). Use the form on the CD to ask the youth how they best relate to Jesus—friend, savior, judge, leader, teacher, example.

DRINKS

" 'Lord, when was it that we saw you...thirsty and gave you something to drink?...' 'Truly, I tell you, just as you did it to one of the least of these' " (Matthew 25:37, 40a).

Service project ideas

COMBO MENU

Main Dishes

Weekly Program Options: *Choose one or all; do in any order. Check each description for variations and the fixin's.*

1. **God Man**—Jesus is God in the flesh (incarnate), yet Jesus is called the Son of God. How can he be the Son if he is God too? How can he be God in the flesh if he also prayed to God? Help your students claim Jesus as God and begin to see the powerful love and grace that God has for humanity.

2. **The Way, the Truth, and the Life**—If we say that Jesus is the only way to heaven, are we not passing judgment on those who do not know or accept Jesus? Help your students see how Jesus' grace and love are meant to bring all of humanity to God, excluding no one.

3. **He's My Friend**—If we can see Jesus as a friend, then perhaps we'll work harder at building a strong relationship with him. Show your students that Jesus is the most trustworthy and dependable friend they could ever imagine.

4. **Savior of the World**—Youth will often parrot the words, "Jesus is my savior" or "Jesus died to save me from my sins." Do they understand what the words mean? How did he save us? Help your students recognize salvation and how they can be used by God to bring salvation to others who are hurt and lost.

Spice It Up

Theme Decorations—*Look at your space. Use your imagination. Why settle for plain when you can go spicy? ("I'll take a taco over skinless chicken any day!") You can give away decorations as prizes at the end of the week or the theme.*

- **Various pictures of Jesus**—Search for "pictures of Jesus" on the Internet (for example, on www.picturesofjesus.com) and print them out or find them in children's Sunday school curriculum. The more pictures, the better the understanding that Jesus has many characteristics that appeal to a diverse people. If you can project the images onto a wall or screen, do so as people are entering the meeting space.

- **Graffiti Wall**—Set up a space on a wall with markers and newsprint or other large paper for youth to write answers to the question, "Who is Jesus to you?" Make it more creative by cutting the paper in the shape of a silhouette of Jesus. You might also add a question each week to the graffiti wall in order to help students focus on the theme.

(Additional ideas on CD)

GOD Man

Have It Your Way!

Choose from, adapt, or rearrange these elements to create the best soul feast for your youth group.

The Fixin's

More fun stuff to make the theme extra special! Your choice.

Munchies

• Crispy Rice Treats

Popular Songs

Use these before and/or after the program to engage the youth. These are some options. Try to include the latest appropriate popular songs.

• "Who Are You?" by The Who (*Then and Now! 1964–2004*)
• "One of Us," by Joan Osborne (*Relish*)
• "I Can Only Imagine," by MercyMe (*Almost There*)

Worship and Praise Music

• "God of Wonders," by Mac Powell (*Worship Together: I Could Sing of Your Love Forever*)
• "Awesome God," by John Tesh (*Worship Collection: Awesome God*)
• "Creed," by Rich Mullins (*Here in America*)
• "Lord of the Dance," by Stephen Curtis Chapman (*Signs of Life*)
• "Breathe," by Christy Nockels (*Worship Together: I Could Sing of Your Love Forever*)

Wall of Super Heroes

Decorate with flair! (Idea on CD)

SOUL FOOD: The best way God could get the message of love across to you and everyone else was by coming here to earth, personally, living out that love for the world first hand.

SCRIPTURE: John 1:1-5, 14 (The Word, which was God, became flesh and dwelt among us.)

Games (Additional game on CD)

Shuffle Your Buns

Have all of the players sit on chairs in a circle. Have one person (It) leave his or her chair and stand in the center.

The object of the game is for the sitting players to prevent It from sitting down. They do this by "shuffling their buns" and moving either left or right to occupy the empty chair before It can sit down. Players may only move one chair to the left or right. Eventually someone isn't fast enough and It is able to sit down. The person on It's left (or right) then becomes It.

Why and Because

Give each person in the group a pen or pencil and an index card. Ask everyone to write a question beginning with the word *why*. Collect the cards. Hand out new cards (a different color card would be helpful here) and ask everyone to write an answer that begins with the word *because*. Collect those cards. Redistribute all the cards at random and have individuals read aloud the questions they receive followed by the answer. Lots of laughs will follow.

Share and Care Groups

Checking in: Highs and lows of the week, prayer requests, and prayer

 Warm up: Together retell the story of Jesus. Invite various youth to contribute pieces of the story from Jesus' birth through the teachings to the Crucifixion and Resurrection. (Additional questions on CD)

Focus Point

Video Option: *The Fifth Element* (1997). In this movie, the incarnation of God is a woman. The parallels between Christ and the main character, Leeloo, are many. She even comes "wrapped in swaddling clothes, lying in a manger." (start: 25:13; stop: 27:50) and saves the world (start:1:57:26; stop: 2:00:08).

Story Options: Read aloud or tell the story "The Birds at Christmas" or the story of the "Prince's Search for Someone to Love" (Stories on CD).

FºCUS THºUGHtS (Text on CD)

Think about God for a moment. Think about your relationship with God. Does God communicate with you? How? What would you imagine might be one of the first things you'll say to God when you get to heaven?

What about Jesus? What is your relationship with him? Do you think differently about Jesus than you think about God? Why? What do you think when you hear that Jesus and God are one and the same?

It's understandable that the idea of God becoming flesh and dwelling among God's people is confusing at times. The church even makes it confusing. We call Jesus the Son of God. We read in Scripture that Jesus is seated at the right hand of God. We know that in the Gospels Jesus prays to God and even says, "My God, why have you forsaken me?" No wonder many Christians (not to mention non-Christians) think of Jesus as a totally separate individual from God. It seems easier to think Jesus as different from God rather than as God deciding to become a human being (God man) and move in with us.

Yet Jesus *is* God in the flesh. Scripture tells us that Jesus was the one through whom the world was created and that God "put on flesh" and came to earth as Jesus. Listen to this Scripture from John, chapter 1. (Read aloud **John 1:1-5, 14.**) When John wrote his Gospel, he wanted everyone to know that when we worship Jesus, we aren't worshiping another god. That would go against the first commandment ("You shall have no other gods before me."). When we celebrate the Trinity (Father, Son, and Holy Spirit), we're not recognizing three individual gods. The Trinity is three particular ways that God, our creator, relates to human beings. When God decided to become a human and live among us, God took on humility and became vulnerable, as vulnerable as a helpless baby.

Think about what that means, though, that Jesus is God in the flesh. What are the implications of the Incarnation? (That's what "God in the flesh means"—*incarnation*.) When God took on flesh and came to be among us, God allowed God's own self to suffer at our hands and to die for us.

God suffered; God died; God overcame death. The Incarnation means that God is not a holy deity who wouldn't understand the struggles of being a teenager. God lived through those struggles. God knows pain and loss and frustration and need and want and desire. God chose to be with us, to experience what we experience, because God loves us.

The Incarnation is also a model of how God can be made "incarnate" in you. As Jesus, God has shown us God's character. As a child of God, you allow God to be made strong in you when you too become a servant, when you forgive, when you love your enemies, when you love your neighbor as you love yourself, and when you love God with all your heart and soul and mind and strength.

God wants this incarnation to continue. God seeks to live out God's character through all God's children, through you. Let's pray.

Other Movie Options

Choose one of these movies, or ask students to recommend a more recent release. Be sure to preview your selection to avoid any content that would be objectionable in your setting. Remember that you must have a video license.
(Video licensing information on CD)

- *Tron* (1982)
- *Sister Act* (1992)
- *Jesus of Montreal* (R) (1990) or various clips from movies about Jesus
- *Face/Off* (R) (1997)
- *Dogma* (R) (1999)

On-the-Street Interviews

Have the youth videotape random youth at the mall (or random church members at various church functions), asking this question: What is the meaning of the word *incarnation*?

Leader Exploration Scripture

- **Philippians 2:5-8** (Christ's humility)
- **Colossians 1:15-16, 19** (Christ's supremacy)

On Screen

Key points from Focus Thoughts (PowerPoint® and Text on CD)

Poster (Design on CD)

Who Do You Say I Am?

Out and About

God became flesh and "moved into the neighborhood." Have your program at a local coffee shop, the mall, or a fast-food place in the neighborhood.

Service Projects

Spend some time "being Jesus" to people in need in your community—a nursing home, a children's home, a hospital emergency waiting room. Play board games with the people there or simply spend time talking and walking with them, treating them like the wonderful creations of God that they are.

⦿ Youth Witness Statement

Ask one or two students to tell about a time they were made certain of God's love for them. (How-to on CD)

FOCUS GROUP

• Why do you think God thought it important to enter into the world as a human being?
• Why would it be important for God to come in humility and vulnerability, rather than in a grandiose style showing strength and power?
• Read aloud **Philippians 2:5-8**. What might have happened if Jesus had decided to "exploit" his equality with God? Which approach attracts you most to God? Why?
• Do God's love and forgiveness have more effect on you than miracles and power? Why or why not?
• How might you allow God's incarnation to be made known through you at school? In your home? With your friends? How might such an incarnation affect those you encounter? How might those affected begin to treat you?

CLOSING

Seeing Christ in One Another

If possible, darken the area and light a candle in the center of the meeting space. Ask the youth and adults to form a circle around the candle. Hand each person an unlit candle. One person should begin by taking the center candle and lighting another person's candle while telling him or her how he or she sees Christ through that person. Next, that person goes to someone else and tells him or her how Christ is evident, and so on, until everyone has a lit candle. Close by telling everyone to take the light of Christ out into the world and be Christ to others.

Read the Scripture Creatively

Turn out all of the lights and have four to six different people read aloud the Scripture from **John 1:1-5, 14** in the dark, using only the light of a penlight or candle. Hearing God's Word repeated over and over again in different voices helps listeners become aware of different emphasis and perspectives. A single light should illuminate the space when "the Word became flesh" is first read.

THE Way, THE TRUTH, AND THE LIFE

SOUL FOOD: In following Jesus we will know God.

SCRIPTURE: John 14:6-7 (Jesus tells the disciples that he is the way, the truth, and the life—and the way to know the Father.)

 **GAMES** (Additional game on CD)

Choices

Ask all of the youth to gather in the center of the room. Call out statements that involve the youth moving to one side or the other of the room if they fit the description. For example: If you are wearing tennis shoes, move to this wall. If you are not, move to that wall. Statements can be factual or just involve opinions.

Newspaper Scavenger Hunt

Divide the group into even teams of three to eight people. Hand each team a stack of newspapers or magazines. Tell the youth that you will call out something they are to find in their newspapers or magazines. When they find what you call, a runner from each group should bring to you a page containing what you called. Announce as you call out each item how many points each item earns, giving higher points to items that are harder to find.

SHARE AND CARE GROUPS

Checking in: Highs and lows of the week, prayer requests, and prayer

Warm up: Talk about these questions: When did you ever feel lost? What did you do? What kinds of precautions do you take to make sure you don't get lost on trips? In strange places? In your choices and decisions? In life?

FOCUS POINT

Video Option: *Secondhand Lions,* 2004. This movie looks at the whole theme of truth and belief. Use the scene where the main character confronts his uncle about the truth he's seeking (Start:1:08:06; stop 1:12:34).

Skit Option: Making a Peanut Butter Sandwich. This is a hilarious stunt that uses one presenter, an audience, a loaf of bread (still in the bag), a jar of peanut butter (unopened), a knife, a plate, a clean place to prepare the sandwich, and washcloth (for cleanup). Be sure to wash hands and do not waste the food.

Have It Your Way!

Choose from, adapt, or rearrange these elements to create the best soul feast for your youth group.

THE FIXIN'S

More fun stuff to make the theme extra special! Your choice.

Munchies

Peanut butter sandwiches (See Skit Option at left.)

Popular Songs

Use these before and/or after the program to engage the youth. These are some options. Try to include the latest appropriate popular songs.

- "Show Me the Way," by Peter Frampton (*Peter Frampton— Greatest Hits*)
- "Step Up to the Microphone," by Newsboys (*Shine: The Hits*)

Worship and Praise Music

- "Step by Step," by Rich Mullins (*Songs 2*)
- "Alive," by P.O.D. (*Satellite*)
- "Praise, Adonai," by Paul Baloche (*Open the Eyes of My Heart*)
- "Shout to the Lord," by Matt Redman (*Worship Together: I Could Sing of Your Love Forever*)
- "I Could Sing of Your Love Forever," by SonicFlood (*Worship Together: I Could Sing of Your Love Forever*)

Other Movie Options

Choose among these movies, or ask students to recommend a more recent release. Be sure to preview your selection to avoid any content that would be objectionable in your setting. You must have a video license. (Video licensing information on CD)

- *O Brother, Where Art Thou?*
- *Signs* (2000)
- *Indiana Jones and the Last Crusade* (1989)
- *Dead Man Walking* (R) (1996)
- *Liar, Liar* (1997)

On-the-Street Interviews

Have the youth videotape random youth at the mall (or random church members at various church functions) giving directions to a well known location.

Leader Background on the Scripture

Find out more about **John 14:6**. (Information on CD)

Leader Exploration Scripture

- **John 10:1-18** (Jesus, the Good Shepherd)
- **John 14:1-14** (Jesus, the Way)

On Screen

Key points from Focus Thoughts (PowerPoint® and Text on CD)

The presenter stands at a table or counter with the items covered and announces, "I am going to do something simple that most everyone here knows how to do. But in order to illustrate to you the importance of communicating and the benefits of actually showing someone how to do something—how helpful it is to be an example of the way to do things—I want you to tell me each and every step in doing this simple task. I will not do anything that you do not tell me to do. Let me say it again, you must be perfectly clear in telling me each step of. . . (*uncover the items with dramatic flair*) making a peanut butter sandwich.*"

As the youth explain each step, the presenter should go out of the way in trying to only do what is specifically stated. For example, when the instruction is given to "take the bread out of the bag" the presenter should rip open the bag and grab all the slices, putting them on the table. When instructions are given to open the peanut butter jar, try banging it on the side of the table in order to open it, or get out a can opener and try using that. When instructions are given to take the peanut butter out of the jar with a knife, use the handle end of the knife. Go overboard with the need for specific, clear instructions.

After the skit you will hand out peanut butter sandwiches for everyone. So as you are preparing the food, handle it appropriately so that it can be eaten. Do not waste food.

FOCUS THOUGHTS (Text on CD)

I enjoy traveling to new places. One of the benefits of being a youth minister is the trips that I get to take my youth on. I enjoy piling everyone into the van and taking off to places unseen to embark on new missions and new experiences.

The youth in my group would tell you though that I usually get them lost. Having never been to our destination, I rely on maps or on what someone has told me. Usually, I get some part of the directions wrong; and we end up turning around and trying another turn or another exit.

There have been a few trips, though, where I did not get us lost. These were the times where I was following someone else who knew the way.

Jesus explained to his disciples that he was going away and that they would one day follow him. They asked, "How can we follow you if we do not know the way?" Jesus' reply was, "I am the way, and the truth, and the life. No one comes to the Father except through me. If you know me, you will know my Father also. From now on you do know him and have seen him" **(John 14:6-7).**

When we seek to find our way to God or when we want to experience God's kingdom, Jesus tells us that all we need do is follow him. Jesus has been there, done that; and he has the t-shirt! We can talk to others, read countless books, listen to sermons, and even read the Bible. If we want to find the true way to God, though, we should follow the one who shows us God best—Jesus.

Too often people take this Scripture and turn it into something that excludes others. They read, "No one comes to the Father except through me" and use that to prove that those who do not follow Christ will never be saved.

18

However, Jesus never intended for "the way" to be some exclusive club, where only those members could get to heaven. Jesus recognized that all people have within them a desire or a need to be with God. Since Jesus is God in the flesh—the embodiment of God (God Man)—he is the best one to guide us to God. In following him, we will no doubt find the way.

Think of it another way. The only way to God is if God allows us near. That's what grace means. We cannot "earn" our way to God, because we are not worthy of being in God's presence. If God were to have mercy, though—if God were to supply ultimate grace and forgiveness—then we could take hold of that grace and claim our place next to God. In order to claim such grace, we must recognize the ultimate example of God's grace—the sacrifice of Jesus who was denied by us, betrayed by us, and put to death for us only to come back to life and still forgive us so that we would know and understand and experience ultimate grace.

Jesus is the way, because there is no better guide than he is to find God. Jesus is the truth, because there is nothing truer than ultimate grace and love. Jesus is the life, because in following him we will discover a life that is far better than any we could ever imagine for ourselves.

FOCUS GROUP

- Talk about a time when you had trouble finding out the truth about something. What did you do to discover the truth? Did it work?
- How important is the truth to you? to your friends?
- In **John 14:6,** Jesus says, "No one comes to the Father except through me." What do you think he means by this? How might someone who is not a Christian hear this? How might it be heard as excluding? How can the statement be heard as inviting?
- Who do you know who needs to hear an invitation to follow Jesus to the Father? How can you make that invitation more inviting?
- Jesus said, "I came that [you] might have life, and have it abundantly" **(John 10:10).** How can a life with Jesus be abundant? How has following Jesus been a blessing to you?

 # CLOSING

Litany (Text on CD)

Tell the youth to respond to the leader's statements in this litany by alternating statements of "You are the way," "You are the truth," and "You are the life."

 # Labyrinth

Check to see if a labyrinth is anywhere nearby. In some areas, mazes are cut into cornfields in early October. Some churches also have labyrinths available for use. If you cannot find one, try making one with lime or chalk on the ground or masking tape in a parking lot or gym floor. (Labyrinth information on CD)

Out and About

Find a one-way road that has a place you could meet that is close to the "one way" sign. Send out postcards before the meeting time with directions to the location where you are meeting—not an address, just directions.

Youth Witness Statement

Ask one or two students to tell about a time in their life when they experienced the feeling of grace from someone else. (How-to on CD)

He's My Friend

Have It Your Way!

Choose from, adapt, or rearrange these elements to create the best soul feast for your youth group.

The Fixin's

More fun stuff to make the theme extra special! Your choice.

Munchies

Have the youth pair up to make an ice cream sundaes. After each pair has constructed a frozen masterpiece, they may eat it together. Have a variety of toppings available.

Popular Songs

Use these before and/or after the program to engage the youth. These are some options. Try to include the latest appropriate popular songs.

- "You've Got a Friend," by James Taylor (*The Best of James Taylor*)
- "Bridge Over Troubled Water," by Simon & Garfunkel (*Simon & Garfunkel*)
- "Whenever I Call You 'Friend,'" by Kenny Loggins (*Yesterday, Today, Tomorrow—The Greatest Hits of Kenny Loggins*)

Worship and Praise Music

- "I Can Only Imagine," by MercyMe (*Almost There*)
- "You Will Never Walk Alone," by Point of Grace (*Free to Fly*)
- "Shout to the North" (*Worship Together: I Could Sing of Your Love Forever*)
- "What a Friend I've Found," by Delirious (*King of Fools*)
- "What a Friend We Have in Jesus"

SOUL FOOD: Only the best friend of all would know every dark secret about you—know your motives, your mistakes, and your misgivings—and still love you and offer you the greatest gift of love. Jesus does all that.

SCRIPTURE: John 4:5-26 (Jesus meets a Samaritan woman at the well, shows her that he knows all about her and accepts her despite her shortcomings.)

 ## Games (Additional game on CD)

Trust Tag

Rules to the usual game of tag apply, except that each player plays this game with a partner and one partner must wear a blindfold. The blindfolded partner's teammate guides him or her by keeping hands on the blindfolded partner's waist and shouting directions. The object is for the blindfolded player to tag another blindfolded player.

Back to Back

Divide your group into pairs and ask them to sit on the floor back-to-back and to link arms. Then tell the pairs to stand up, without letting go of their partner's arms. It can be done if the two work together. Once everyone has it figured out, combine two pairs into a foursome, have the foursomes sit on the floor with their backs together and their arms linked. Tell the foursomes to stand up. It's a little more difficult. Keep adding more people to the groups until the youth can't stand up anymore.

Share and Care Groups

Checking in: Highs and lows of the week, prayer requests, and prayer

Warm up: Tell the group your ideas of the qualities of the ultimate friend. Or talk about these questions:

- What is the best thing you have ever done for a friend? Why did you do that?
- Would you do it again? Why?
- If you could have done that without the friend knowing that it was you, would you still do it? Why?

Focus Point

Video Option: *The Fisher King* (R) (1991). Use the last scene around the friendship that developed between Perry and Jack (start: 2:12:40; stop: at the ending credits).

Photo Option: Try to get photos of your youth being with their friends. You might surprise them by collecting the photos from their parents before the meeting time, or you might invite the youth to bring their photos on their own. If your youth group takes a lot of photos, make this a time that you will get out all of the old photos from youth gatherings and trips. Spend some time just sitting and looking at all the fun times spent with friends. Play some of the music selections in the background.

If you can get the photos in advance, invite a "techie" student to scan them and create a PowerPoint® slide show.

 ## Focus Thoughts (Text on CD)

Jesus is tired and thirsty. It's around lunchtime, and he's waiting at the well just outside a Samaritan city. He's sitting there alone because the disciples have gone into the city to get food for lunch. Not many people come to the well this time of day, so this is a quiet place for Jesus to rest.

A woman arrives there, though. She is alone, and she is from the city. According to the customs of the day, since she is a Samaritan and a woman, Jesus should not talk to her. He should have nothing to do with her. He is a Jew. She is a Samaritan and a woman who is a stranger. They both know that they are not to communicate with each other.

However, Jesus is tired and thirsty. The woman has a bucket to get water, and Jesus tells the woman to give him a drink.

This may be difficult to understand today; but the woman is very surprised that Jesus would even speak to her, not to mention that he would ask her for a drink. They strike up a conversation, and he tells her that he is the source of the living water that quenches all thirst. If she were to drink of this living water, then she would never need anything again.

The woman is now intrigued. She would love to have some of this water. Then she would not have to keep coming to this well each day. The woman, you see, is shunned by her community. She comes to the well after everyone else has gone because she is embarrassed; she's an outcast. Why is she an outcast? Listen and you will hear.

Jesus tells the woman to go into the city and get her husband, and he will tell both of them about the living water. The woman tells Jesus that she has no husband. That's when Jesus begins telling her things that he would not normally know. He says that she is right to say that she has no husband. She has, in fact, had five husbands; and the man she is with now is not her husband. For this reason she is ashamed. This is why the woman does not feel welcome by the rest of her community.

The woman realizes that this Jew, whose culture and religion told him not to associate with her, chose to speak with her. This Jew not only spoke with her, he also offered her an everlasting gift of living water. This Jew not only spoke with her and offered her life-giving water, but he also knows all about

 ## Other Movie Options

Choose one of these, or ask students to recommend a more recent release. Be sure to preview your selection to avoid any content that would be objectionable in your setting. Remember you must have a video license.
(Video licensing information on CD)

- *Simon Birch* (1998)
- *Tuesdays With Morrie* (1999)
- *Rudy* (1993)
- *The Shawshank Redemption* (R) (1994)

On-the-Street Interviews

Have the youth videotape random youth at the mall (or random church members at various church functions). Ask this question: What are characteristics of the best friend ever?

Along With the Message

In advance, invite two youth to work with you to dramatize the story of the woman at the well as you tell it. Have the youth wear costumes or don't.

Leader Exploration Scripture

- **John 15:1-17** (Jesus, the True Vine)

Service Project

Befriend someone. Look around your neighborhood and your school. As you begin to see others through Christ-eyes, you will likely find someone who needs a friend. Put your own friendship skills to work. Invite him or her to youth group too. (Take on this effort on as a commitment, but be sure that you don't treat your new friend as a "project.")

Out and About

Have the group climb a wall. Find a wall that is about 10 feet high, without cracks or holes. Make sure that it is at a place where people can gather on top as well as around the bottom (like a roof, a catwalk, or a dirt bank as in a retaining wall). Bring cushions or mats to place around the bottom of the wall. Be alert to safety issues. Get permission to use the wall and permission forms for the youth.

Have the youth gather at the bottom of the wall, then tell them that they are to get everyone over the top of the wall. They must work together, and they should be affirming and supportive throughout the whole process. Make sure there are extra adults to act as spotters to stop anyone from getting hurt. Your group may need to break into smaller teams to do this activity or meet at various "walls" around town.

After the activity, talk about the way affirmation, encouragement, and support help us make it over the walls in our own lives.

Youth Witness Statement

Ask one or two students to talk about how Jesus is a friend of theirs. (How to on CD.)

Make a Friendship Bracelet

Collect beads and some cool string or twine and allow some time for youth to make friendship bracelets in honor of their friend Jesus. Ask them to make them in such a way that they will be reminded of the friend they have in Jesus.

her—and still he offers her so much. He is a stranger, but he knows her and accepts her. I can think of no better friend than this.

Jesus said in **John 15:13** that the greatest love a person can have for another is to lay down his life for his friend. Jesus has done that for each of us.

Jesus, who is God in the flesh—God Man—pays attention to me and to you. He offers me (and you) life-giving water even though he knows our every weakness, our every sin, our every shameful action, our every shortcoming. He knows us entirely, yet he died for us so that we may live with his love.

This is a friend. This is a true, ultimate friend. This is the only friend I can truly trust in every way.

FOCUS GROUP (Additional questions on CD)

- What do you know about the way Jesus' friends treated him? How did Jesus respond?
- What would you do if you found out that a best friend was doing something harmful to himself or herself? Would you risk your friendship? Why, or why not?
- What if the roles were swapped and a best friend of yours told your parents or your youth leader whether you were doing something harmful to yourself? Would you be glad or upset that he or she told someone? Why?
- In **John 15:12,** Jesus says, "This is my commandment, that you love one another as I have loved you." What does this say about how to treat your friends? your enemies?

CLOSING

Circle Benediction

Ask the group to stand in a circle, facing inward. Have them wear their friendship bracelets, if they have made them.

Tell them to cross their arms in front of them (right arm over left). As they do so, explain that their arms form a cross over their hearts, reminding them of Jesus' call to give up our lives to him—just as he gave his very life for us, his friends.

Then ask the group to join hands (while their arms are still crossed). This is to remind them that all are linked together through Christ.

Finally, ask two people in this circle to let go of their grip, forming a gap in the circle. This is to remind them that Jesus is a part of the group, that he is present with them, and that the group is not closed but should always be open to others.

While in this formation, close with this benediction from **Numbers 6:24-26:**

> May the Lord bless you and keep you. May the Lord make his face to shine upon you and be gracious unto you. May the Lord lift up his countenance upon you and give you peace.

Savior of the World

SOUL FOOD: A savior is someone who saves you from something terrible. Christ offers you salvation from being separated from God forever.

SCRIPTURE: John 3:16-17 (God so loved the world)

 Games (Additional games on CD)

Picture It

Divide the group into teams of two to six. Have the teams move as far away from one another as possible. The leader is in the center of the room and holds a stack of cards with about twenty words or phrases written on them. As the game begins, one member from each team runs to the center, looks at the phrase or word written on the top card, and runs back to his or her team. That person picks up a drawing pad and a pen and draws images to help teammates guess the word or phrase. No words can be written or spoken by the runner/artist. Give higher points for more difficult words or phrases.

Memorize It

Write **John 3:16** on slips of paper in two-word phrases; put the slips in balloons and then blow up the balloons. Hand out the balloons as students arrive. If you have a large group, use different color balloons for a set of the phrases. At "Go" students find their "set" and put the verse in order. Award prizes. Have the group repeat the verse several times.

SHARE AND CARE GROUPS

Checking in: Highs and lows of the week, prayer requests, and prayer

Warm up: Ask the group to list some of the things about our world (and their lives) that prove we need to be saved from something.

FOCUS POINT

Video Options: Use several clips that show people being saved from peril or where the hero cleans up the evil. Here are some possibilities:

- *Titanic* (1997) (Start 2:05:24—"Jack! Will this work?" to 2:06:27—"You did it!")
- *Backdraft* (R) (1991) (Start 51:56—"My baby! Please, my baby's in there!" to 54:12—The hero has rescued the boy from the burning room.)
- *Forrest Gump* (1995) (Start 53:37—Forrest goes back into the jungle to save a friend's life to 54:22—Jungle explodes behind Forrest Gump.)

Have It Your Way!

Choose from, adapt, or rearrange these elements to create the best soul feast for your youth group.

THE FIXIN'S

More fun stuff to make the theme extra special! Your choice.

Munchies

Give everyone a roll of Life Saver candies to remind them of Christ as Savior.

Popular Songs

Use these before and/or after the program to engage the youth. These are some options. Try to include the latest appropriate popular songs.

- "You Raise Me Up," by Josh Groban (*Closer*)
- "My Sacrifice," by Creed (*Weathered*)
- "Some Kind of Wonderful," by the Drifters (*The Very Best of the Drifters*)
- "Pride (In the Name of Love)" by U2 (*The Best of 1980–1990*)
- "I Would Die 4 U," by Prince (*The Hits 2*)
- "In Your Eyes," by Peter Gabriel (*So*)

Worship and Praise Music

- "Spoken For," by MercyMe (*Spoken For*)
- "You Are My King (Amazing Love)" by Newsboys (*Adoration: Worship Album*)
- "What a Friend I've Found," by Delirious (*King of Fools*)
- "Grace Like Rain," by Todd Agnew (*Grace Like Rain*)
- "There's Something About That Name," by Sonic Flood/Kevin Max (*Listen Louder*)

💿 Other Movie Options

Choose one of these movies, or ask students to recommend a more recent release. Be sure to preview your selection to avoid any content that would be objectionable in your setting. Remember you must have a video license.
(Video licensing information on CD)

• *The Matrix* (R) (1999)
• *A Simple Plan* (R) (1998)
• *Star Wars—Episode I, The Phantom Menace* (1999)
• *Schindler's List* (R) (1993)

On-the-Street Interviews

Have the youth videotape random youth at the mall (or random church members at various church functions). Ask this question: What is worth giving your life for?

Out and About

Tell your group to meet at a fire station. Call at least a week beforehand to schedule a tour of the station. Don't forget to schedule an interview time with those who give their lives saving people from dangerous situations. Prepare some questions in advance.

💿 FOCUS THOUGHTS (Text on CD)

Sin is something that we are all guilty of. It's something that we've all done. Anytime you have gone against God's will, you have sinned.

Such sin in our life tends to make us feel guilty. We recognize, especially when we are faced with total, complete perfection, that we are guilty of doing something wrong. Something that is wrong does not fit with perfection.

Anytime you have something perfect, it makes the imperfect thing look and feel out of place. An engine that is running perfectly will begin to run poorly if a dirty filter is put in place of the clean one. A piece of art that I draw or paint would be terribly out of place in a museum of fine art. A wrong note played in a perfect musical masterpiece would be out of place. In the same way, when we, who are imperfect, one day come before God's throne and are in God's very presence, will recognize that we do not fit. Our sin has caused us to stand out and make what is perfect no longer perfect. In such a case, we will know guilt. Our sin, when set against God's perfection, will show us our guilt.

But God does not want that guilt to stop us from coming to such perfection. God wants to say, "Look, you are invited to be with me. I want you with me."

Do you know the story of the Fall in Genesis? Do you remember how Adam and Eve reacted to God's presence when they heard God coming into the garden after they had sinned?

Adam and Eve had just eaten the forbidden fruit that God had told them not to eat. They sinned, because they did the one thing God had told them not to do. That evening, when God came to walk in the garden, they hid. They knew that they had done something wrong. When God's presence was known, their first response was to hide from such perfection. The guilt humanity feels pushes and pulls us away from the perfection of God.

That's why God knew that a savior was needed. Somehow *God* had to save us from our guilt—we couldn't do it ourselves. In order for us to recognize that we could stand before God faultless and blameless again, God had to save us. That's what it means to be "saved from our sins."

So God saw that a sacrifice was needed—again, not because of God's rule, but because we, in our guilt, would be unable to come before God until such guilt was paid for. The only payment that would wipe away such guilt would be if one of us, a human being, were to be perfect and yet pay the price for our sins. It would have to be done willingly because that's what a sacrifice means—to willingly give something up.

The problem was, there were no perfect human beings. Humanity was sinful. Not one was without sin. Imagine the sorrow of God—to want so much to be able to lovingly hold you in God's arms, but you were so imperfect and full of guilt that you could never feel totally welcome in God's presence. Imagine how sad God must have felt when God recognized that humanity was lost to paradise.

A sacrifice, then, would be necessary. The only one who was perfect was God. That meant that God would have to become a human (the Incarnation, remember) and move into our neighborhood. The God/Man Jesus would remain perfect and without sin and then willingly give his life as a sacrifice for the sins of the entire world. God threw in a little twist too. God would overcome death itself. Jesus would live again!

Because of Jesus' death and Resurrection, we can be guilt-free before God. We are forgiven of the worst sin we could ever imagine.

That is how Jesus is your Savior. That is how Jesus saves you from sin and guilt. He has allowed himself to be sacrificed by his own people—by the ones he loves—and come back to life to live eternally with God. He is God, but he is also human. He has died, but he came back to life so that you would know that you are forgiven and that God allows you to stand or sit or kneel or jump for joy in God's presence. No longer will you feel out of place before God, because someone who was perfect willingly gave himself as payment for your sin.

Jesus saves you by helping you realize that your sin can no longer separate you from God. He did that for the entire world because he loves the entire world. Read aloud **John 3:16-17.**

From the very beginning, humanity has sinned and, like Adam and Eve, felt the separation from God that sin causes. But Jesus' sacrifice shows us— shows you—the way to salvation. Jesus has shown us that he is God; he has shown us that he is the way, the truth, and the life. Jesus has shown you that he is your friend who loves you and accepts you no matter what you do; and Jesus has shown you the way to being saved is by accepting his sacrifice, presenting yourself before God, and acknowledging Jesus Christ as your savior. Jesus makes salvation possible; the gift is waiting for you to claim it.

 ## FOCUS GROUP (Additional questions on CD)

• Who do you know who needs to hear the good news about salvation?
• How can you thank God for sending Jesus as your savior?

 ## CLOSING

Altar Time

As you can, emphasize what knowing Christ has done for you. An appropriate Scripture is **John 9:25** ("One thing I do know, that though I was blind, now I see."). It is not as important to define Christ in theological terms as it is to let Christ change our lives. The only way we can understand Christ is to encounter him and to experience his power in our life. Invite the youth to enter into a personal relationship with Jesus Christ.

Encourage the youth to come to the altar for a prayer time; allow them to leave when they are ready. Play appropriate music in the background. Be available for personal conversations immediately afterward. Or note who may need a call during the week for follow up.

 ### Guided Meditation (Text on CD)

Service Projects

Help the youth decide on a place or places in your community where your group can serve others—a soup kitchen, a homeless shelter, a playground where they can spend the day with some needy kids. Talk about what kinds of ways God was using you to "save" those you reached.

Plan a "Rescue Party." Help the group brainstorm ways the youth can be involved in helping Jesus transform the world. Think of the environment, showing kindness to those areas that need a little tenderness, and breaking through racial or economic barriers in your community through playing, working or worshiping together.

Youth Witness Statement

Ask one or two youth to talk about their own personal account of a rescue that changed a way of living—a bad family situation was changed, a wrong attitude or habit was dropped, someone pointed out a wrong understanding which changed a whole outlook on life. (How-to on CD)

PICTURE THIS!

DO YOU SEE IT?

How do you picture yourself? The images we hold of ourselves provide us with information about who we are and, consequently, direct our actions. Yet God is about making us new creations. Do we see God at work in our lives? Are we able to see ourselves as called, grace-full, forgiven, and devoted? These images are picture-perfect.

 APPETIZERS (Additional ideas on CD)

Publicity Ideas: *Select any or all of the ideas below. Combine or simplify. Use your imagination. Invite a team of youth to decide how to personalize each program. Create a timeline for maximum effect. Spread the word with passion.*

☺ Take candid shots of youth around the church. Create a collage of the photos, leaving an empty space for one more photos. Put a caption on it that says, "Picture Yourself Here!" Give details on where and when the first session will meet. Do a large poster size for display; use a copier to shrink the size and make copies. Send the copies to members and prospects; give extras to youth in your group to give to their friends.

☺ Buy a jigsaw puzzle. Send one piece of the puzzle to each member of your group, with a note that says, "Come to (location) at (time) on (date) to find out how your piece of the puzzle fits in our picture!" As youth arrive with their puzzle piece, have the puzzle in place so that they can add their piece and see the complete picture. If everyone does not attend, the youth will see how incomplete a group can really be without all members.

☺ Create "Wanted" posters of youth who have not been around much lately. Assign them fake crimes for which they are guilty, such as "Guilty of Not Being Around Much" or "Guilty of Leaving Us Waiting." Include hair and eye color information and post a reward. A free movie pass to anyone who can get this person to come to the next event will give a little motivation to everyone.

☺ Have someone take a photo of you or one of your youth in a "touristy-type" pose. Make multiple 4-by-6 copies of the picture, glue them to a 4-by-6 index card, and mail one to each youth as you would a postcard. Put all of the details for your upcoming meetings on the back.

DRINKS

" 'Lord, when was it that we saw you . . . thirsty and gave you something to drink? . . .' 'Truly, I tell you, just as you did it to one of the least of these' " (Matthew 25:37, 40a).

Service project ideas

COMBOS MENU

Main Dishes

Weekly Program Options: *Choose one or all; do in any order. Check each description for the fixin's.*

1. **Picture Yourself Called**—Why does God call us? How do we hear that call?

2. **Picture Yourself Grace-Full**—What is this special gift that God gives so freely? Why is it so difficult for us to understand and accept?

3. **Picture Yourself Forgiven**—How could anyone forgive someone who had betrayed him three times? How are we supposed to live up to that kind of example?

4. **Picture Yourself Devoted**—What kind of person was Ruth that she could place the needs of Naomi above her own? What can we learn from such models of devotion?

Spice It Up (Additional ideas on CD)

Theme Decorations: *Look at your space. Use your imagination! Why settle for plain when you can go spicy? Remember, you can give away decorations as prizes at the end of the week or the theme.*

- Decorate your meeting space with photos. Gather photos of your youth, volunteers, and youth group adventures. Add photos of special places and photos that challenge youth to respond, such as those from newsmagazines or nature magazines. Frame them, make collages of them, hang or stand them individually, enlarge them (copy machines are great for this), stick them in odd places. Hang different photos each week. Have fun with the decor.

- Put some students to work on their computers to create an image of one person from the facial features taken from several students' photos. Have a guessing contest as students arrive. Award a prize.

- Lots of teens have cameras or those nifty little phones with picture-taking capability, so why not use that to your advantage? As you're preparing for this theme, send a few students out, with instructions to record as many instances as they can find of "ah-ha" moments, moments when they see people really demonstrating what it means to be called, full of grace, forgiven, or devoted. Download all the photos and make (better yet, assign this task to one of your youth) a PowerPoint® presentation for your last night of worship together. Let the images be the culminating point of the entire theme. Set the presentation to music such as "Defining Moment," by Newsong, to create an "ah-ha" moment all its own! (See Closing on page 39.)

- Start a new tradition. Take a photo of your whole group, label it "Class of _____," frame it and display it prominently in your church hallway where everyone can enjoy it.

- Have a photo scavenger hunt. (Instructions on CD)

- Give out a special wristband to each youth for every program they attend. Award prizes to the youth who attend all four programs and who still have all four of their wristbands.

Picture Yourself Called

Have It Your Way!

Choose from, adapt, or rearrange these elements to create the best soul feast for your youth group.

The Fixin's

More fun stuff to make the theme extra special! Your choice.

Munchies

Who's calling? Can you hear? Try these for snacks with a message:

- Wax Lips (can be purchased in most discount stores)
- Elephant Ears (similar to funnel cakes)
- Bugles™ (snack crackers)

Popular Songs

Use these before and/or after the program to engage the youth. These are some options. Try to include the latest appropriate popular songs.

- "Call Me," by Petula Clark (*Ultimate Petula Clark*)
- "Wait for an Answer," by Heart (*Bad Animals*)
- "A Sense of Wonder," by Van Morrison (*A Sense of Wonder*)
- "Help," by the Beatles (*Help*)
- "Part of the Plan, by Dan Fogelberg (*Greatest Hits*)

Worship and Praise Music

- "Word of God Speak," by MercyMe (*Spoken For*)
- "Breathe on Me," by Jennifer Knapp (*Way I Am*)
- "The Invitation," by Steven Curtis Chapman (*Speechless*)

SOUL FOOD: Jesus calls each of us to follow him. We need to be listening and ready to respond.

SCRIPTURE: Luke 5:1-11 (Jesus calls Simon Peter, James, and John)

 Games

Telephone With a Twist (Questionnaire on CD)

First hand out copies of "My Favorites" questionnaire to the youth for them to note their favorites. The first space is for them to put their name; the rest of the spaces are for them to put their favorites of the listed categories. Use the information on these sheets to play the classic game where you whisper a sentence into one person's ear and that person has to repeat to the next person what he or she heard, who passes it on, and so forth. The last person has to tell what he or she heard. You'll learn a little more about one another when you tell what the sentence was supposed to be.

Roll Call (Handout on CD)

In this fun game, each person gets a silly new name that sticks with him or her throughout the whole meeting. Using the "Roll Call" list on the CD, assign names according to the letters of each person's name. Be sure to call them those names all day long.

Share and Care Groups

Checking in: Highs and lows of the week, prayer requests, and prayer

Warm up: Do you like talking on the telephone? What is your personal telephone style—to get on and talk for hours or to get on and off quickly? Who is your favorite person to talk with on the phone? Has anyone ever hung up on you? What were the circumstances? How did it make you feel? Have you ever hung up on anyone? (Additional questions on CD)

Focus Point

Video Option: *Frequency* (2000) (Start at approximately 47:14 and run to approximately 53:22). John and his dad are conversing about life in general, neither wanting to cut the call short. Be sure to preview the selection to avoid any content that would be objectionable in your setting. Remember that you must have a video license. (Video licensing information on CD)

Skit Option: Have a group of youth write and perform a skit about God calling on the telephone. Use cell phones or really jazz it up by staging it with a phone booth. Suggested topics might include God calling when it's inconvenient, God calling and you don't recognize who it is, and God calling and no one answers. An alternative is to incorporate skits into the Focus Thoughts outline. (See below.)

FOCUS THOUGHTS (Outline & suggestions on CD)

Outline

1. Jesus Christ is constantly calling us to follow him, but often we don't hear his call. Many things can keep us from hearing the call, such as busyness, lack of faith, and mixed-up priorities. Does Christ get a busy signal? Do we hang up on him? Do we totally ignore the ring and not answer at all?

2. Even when we hear Christ's call, we don't always choose to respond to it. It may appear too difficult, or we may feel unqualified or unworthy for the task. Yet Jesus chose sinners and outcasts as his disciples. God's loving grace makes us worthy to be chosen.

3. Hearing Jesus' call isn't enough; the response is equally important. Amazement isn't enough. Christ calls us to action. In the case of the three fishermen, the response involved pulling up their nets, leaving everything else, and following Jesus. And their lives were infinitely richer for doing so.

4. Everyone is called by God in some way. Are you listening?

Let's pray.

FOCUS GROUP (Additional questions on CD)

Read aloud **Luke 5:1-11.** (Three disciples respond to God's call.)

- What do you think Simon was thinking when Jesus told him to go out into the water and drop the nets?
- Although the men had been fishing all night and not caught anything, when Jesus told them to drop the nets, suddenly they caught a lot. Was that a miracle? If so, what would have been Jesus' motive for making it happen?
- Why did Simon Peter tell Jesus to go away from him?
- Why did they have to leave everything behind?
- Does God call us to leave things behind? What do you think God might want us to let go of?
- Have you ever felt God calling you? If so, how did you know it was God? How did you respond?
- What do you think might be keeping you from hearing God's call in your life?

Guest Speakers

- Invite your pastor to talk to the group about listening for a call into the ministry. Direct students who are interested in exploring further a call to ministry to www.plse.org and www.IsGodCallingYou.org.

- Invite a career counselor to talk to the group about their future. Have him or her talk about how your gifts and ambitions should be tied into what you are called to do.

(Additional idea on CD)

Leader Scripture Exploration

- **Exodus 3:1-6a** (Moses and the burning bush)
- **Jonah 1:1–3:10** (Jonah runs away)
- **Luke 1:46-55** (Mary's response to her call)
- **Acts 9:1-19a** (Saul's conversion)

Out and About

Go to a large field and use a megaphone. Call each youth by name to come join you in the bleachers to talk about God's call.

Service Projects

- Design a youth directory. Make a page for each person, including pertinent information such as name, address, phone number, grade, siblings, hobbies, and favorite Bible verse. Photos of each person add a nice touch too.

- Set up a phone collection station. Let people donate their old cell phones to be given to the local spousal abuse shelter.

(Additional ideas on CD)

Stay-in-Touch Extras

• Construct a telephone "tree" for disseminating important information for all youth.

• Develop a youth prayer chain by recruiting youth who would agree to receive a phone call from one person about a specific prayer request, pray about the request individually, and then phone another person to keep the chain going.

• Set up a telephone answering machine on the youth phone line to make important information available to all youth. Post messages about upcoming events or adjustments to schedules.

• Purchase an inexpensive beeper to be passed around to youth who are going through difficult times. Let all the youth have the number to the beeper so they can call that person. The "beeper carriers" will hear/feel the beep and know that someone is thinking of them and praying for them. Think how reassuring it would be to someone who just lost his grandmother to be beeped by friends to let him know others are praying for him! (Cautionary note: Youth need to understand that this is not a game but can be a powerful tool for letting others know you and others care about them. If misuse occurs, simply remove the beeper from usage for a short period.)

(Additional ideas on CD)

CLOSING

Can You Hear Me Now?

Gather a variety of telephones and set up an altar table with them.

With the help of one of your parents or a youth counselor, stage a phone call in which God calls you because God's having trouble getting through to the youth. Let the youth hear God say how much God loves them and wishes to have more time with them. (Set up worship in an auditorium or large room where you have the capability to use a sound system without being seen.)

Reread the Scripture, this time from a shorter version (**Matthew 4:18-22**). Remind the youth that listening for God and then responding to the call can provide major "ah-ha" moments in their lives and that following Jesus is a great and wonderful adventure.

Close with a youth benediction such as **Numbers 6:24-26.**

Prayer Path (Prayer Path stations on CD)

Create individual "ah-ha" moments for your youth with a prayer path activity. Invite the youth to walk the path as part of the closing (although each must walk through the path individually).

Because the Prayer Path stations refer to each of the themes (called, devoted, forgiven, grace-full), you may choose to use it later in the series or multiple times during the series. You may also modify the idea and direct the youth to only one station each week.

Or set up the Prayer Path and have it available at various times throughout the week for youth to participate at their own convenience. If you take the latter option, you may want to have youth sign up for specific times.

PiCTURE YOURSELF GRACE-FULL

SOUL FOOD: Nothing we can ever do will make us worthy of God's love, but God offers us the incredible gift of grace.

SCRIPTURE: Luke 15:11-32 (the story of two sons)

Games

Earn It! (Questions on CD)

Using the handy-dandy set of questions provided for you on the CD, find out how much the youth know about some of our best-loved Bible stories and about grace. Divide the youth into four groups, and promise the winning group some kind of cool prize. Give them a few minutes to come up with team names, and then start the game. Call out a question. The first team to answer correctly gets a point; the team with the most points at the end of the game wins! Here's the rub: After playing and then awarding the prize to the winning team, hand out more prizes to ALL the players. See how your group feels about this sudden display of grace to the losers!

Gracefully Yours

No one looks graceful with some of these relays! Divide your group into smaller relay teams using an idea from "How to Group Youth" (on the CD). Then try relay races with these ideas or creative ones or your own:

- Tie each person's knees together.
- Tie one person's ankles to those of another.
- Have the players do the crab walk (on all fours with their back facing the ground).
- Pair players back to back, with their arms linked.
- Pair players to do the polka (Never seen a youth look graceful doing that!)
- Players ride piggyback.

SHARE AND CARE GROUPS

Checking in: Highs and lows of the week, prayer requests, and prayer

Warm up: What does it mean when you say someone is really graceful? In addition to being graceful physically, what are other examples of being filled with grace or being gracious? Work together to come up with a definition of grace. (Additional questions on CD)

Have It Your Way!

Choose from, adapt, or rearrange these elements to create the best soul feast for your youth group.

The Fixin's

More fun stuff to make the theme extra special! Your choice.

Munchies

Again, it's not so much the actual food but how it's served that will make the point in this lesson! Here are some ideas sure to help drive the point home:

- Let everyone fix a plate for someone else.

- Better yet, why not get together and make cookies. Save some to serve each other but then place the others out on a plate on Sunday morning before church for everyone to enjoy!

- Don't serve enough. Intentionally run out of something and then watch to see who shows grace to someone else by giving their own food away. Don't let that go unnoticed. Be sure to talk about it! (Even if a person deliberately doesn't share, it will still be a good lesson!)

- Invite parents to join you for your snack time. Have the youth serve the parents (not necessarily their own parents).

Popular Songs

Use these before and/or after the program to engage the youth. These are some options. Try to include the latest appropriate popular songs.

- "Leader of the Band," by Dan Fogelberg (*Dan Fogelberg—Greatest Hits*)

Worship and Praise Music

- "Amazing Grace" (sung to the tune of "Peaceful, Easy Feeling" or its traditional tune)
- "Wesleyan Grace," (sung to traditional tune or to the tune of one of these: *Gilligan's Island* theme song, *Adam's Family* theme song, *Jeopardy* theme song, Army Boot Camp Call)

Leader Scripture Exploration

- **Romans 3:23-26** (All have sinned.)
- **Romans 6:1-2** (Should we continue in sin?)
- **2 Corinthians 9:8** (God provides so that you may share.)
- **2 Corinthians 12:9** (God's grace is sufficient.)
- **Ephesians 2:8-10** (By grace we are saved and prepared for good works.)

Out and About

Initiate an evangelistic effort for your church by designing door hangers. Get the youth to take them door to door as a group activity; then celebrate a job well done with some snacks back at church!

(Additional ideas on CD)

Focus Point

Video Option: In the movie *Radio* (2003), the coach sees Radio standing at the fence, watching the football team practice. The coach tells his assistant to go over with a bottle of water. The assistant coach questions doing so, but does it anyway. (Start: 20:35; stop: 22:25.) Be sure to preview your selection to avoid any content that would be objectionable in your setting. Remember that you must have a video license. (Video licensing information on CD)

Activity Option: Who's the Real Winner? (Handout on CD) The only way to really win this game is to accept the gift of grace. Using the checklist found on the CD, have each youth figure out the points he or she is worth today. Promise a big prize to the person who comes up with more than 100 points. When points are all tallied and no winners found (and there won't be, trust me), award everyone a prize. (Careful, there could be some grunting about playing stupid unfair games here.)

Then dive into a discussion using the following questions:

- Why do you think no one won?
- How hard was it to win this game? Was it even possible?
- How does this compare to the "game of life"?
- Why do we keep trying to impress God or earn God's love?
- Is it even possible?
- How does it make you feel to know that everyone wins in the end?

Focus Thoughts (Outline on CD)

Outline

For many people, the idea of grace is difficult to grasp. Some of us think that we need to earn God's favor. We see ourselves as unworthy of such great love. Others simply don't recognize and claim the gift that is offered.

Key Points:

1. No one in the world can love us like God does. God loves us regardless of whether we're happy or sad, sinful or pure, lovable or unlovable. None of us are able to do anything to earn God's love. No works are big enough. We can't earn God's love. God simply offers it.

2. And yet many of us have trouble accepting that love. We don't understand that kind of love. It's not "human."

3. Some of us live in such ways that we *know* that we don't deserve to be loved. Some of us simply *feel* unworthy. Some of us try to live in such ways that we think will be approved of by God. We think we deserve God's love because we've earned it by being good.

4. But earning and deserving have nothing to do with how God loves us. God offers us the gift of grace simply because God loves us and desires the best for us. This gift is free. We must decide, like the two brothers, whether we will accept it.

# FOCUS GROUP (Additional questions on CD)

Read aloud **Luke 15:11-32.**

Use these questions to help the participants be clear about the story. Or invite them to do a round-robin retelling of the story in their own words.

- What did the younger son do after he got his money?
- After he spent all the money, how did the son live?
- When the son realized his own foolishness, what did he do?
- How did the younger son expect the father to respond? What actually happened?
- How did the older son feel about the celebration? Why?
- What did the father tell the older son about what he too could have?

Use these questions to make life connections:

- With whom do you identify more? the younger son or the older son?
- Why do we insist on the need for things to be fair?
- What surprised you about the father's answer to the older son? What do you think the older son will do? Why?
- When was the last time you received a great gift that you didn't think you deserved? What was it? Why didn't you deserve it?
- Why do we feel the need to earn our rewards?
- How does that compare to this story?
- What do you think is God's message for those of us who identify with the younger son? What do you think is God's message for those of us who identify with the older son?
- Why do you think God wants to give us grace?

# CLOSING

Accepting the Gift

On the altar for worship, place a small wrapped box (you can probably get small jewelry boxes donated by a local store) for each youth. The boxes can be empty, because they are strictly symbolic. Remind the youth that the gift of grace is free. We don't have to do anything to earn it; but you do have to accept it as a gift of love from God.

Have someone play "Amazing Grace" on the guitar as students come forward and take a box. Tell the youth to place these wrapped boxes somewhere they will be seen every day as a constant reminder of this incredible gift.

Prayer Path

Close with the Prayer Path, or remind the youth of the times during the week it will be available for them. (Prayer Path stations on CD)

Service Projects

Send the youth out on a day of Random Acts of Kindness. Give them the instructions to go do nice things for people who don't ask for them, aren't expecting them, and don't even know the youth. Be sure to tell the youth to be secretive about it; after all, they're not doing it for recognition or fame—strictly to show grace to someone else. Some suggestions:

- Go through the drive-through at your favorite fast food restaurant and pay for the car behind you; then drive away.

- Pull up to a house with a yard that needs raking, jump out, rake as fast as you can, and then leave.

- Wash windshields in the parking lot of a local store. Be subtle so that your work goes unnoticed until the people are ready to drive away.

- You get the idea. The sky's the limit!

Be sure to schedule a Random Acts of Kindness celebration back at the church after everyone is finished so you can report on the good works that you each did and rejoice that you all worked together to show grace.

PICTURE YOURSELF FORGIVEN

HAVE IT YOUR WAY!
Choose from, adapt, or rearrange these elements to create the best soul feast for your youth group.

THE FIXIN'S
More fun stuff to make the theme extra special! Your choice.

Munchies

• S'Mores (<u>Recipe on CD</u>).
As the youth cook and feast on the S'mores, talk about forgiveness. Remind them that as a simple graham cracker and chocolate bar are transformed into something mouth-watering and delicious, so they too can be transformed into something even better by allowing forgiveness to work in their lives. It brings us to a better conclusion than living with vengefulness and grudges.

• Tamale Cheese Dip (<u>Recipe on CD</u>)
• Forgotten Cookies (<u>Recipe on CD</u>)
• A box of fancy chocolates (almost always good for making an apology)

Popular Songs

Use these before and/or after the program to engage the youth. These are some options. Try to include the latest appropriate popular songs.

• "E-mail My Heart," by Britney Spears (*Baby, One More Time*)
• "Moment of Forgiveness," by Indigo Girls (*Become You*)
• "Bridge Over Troubled Waters," by Simon and Garfunkel (*Simon and Garfunkel's Greatest Hits*)

SOUL FOOD: Forgiveness is hard for us, but Jesus shows us a better way to live.

SCRIPTURE: John 21:15-19 (Jesus forgives Peter.)

Games

Cups O'Fun

Divide the youth into two or more equal teams, each lined up in a straight line, with approximately 10–15 feet between each person. Each person in line should hold a small paper cup. At the end of each line, place a bucket of water. At the other end of each line, place an empty two-liter soda bottle (lid off). On "go," the person closest to the bucket fills his or her cup with water, runs to the next person in line, dumps it into his or her cup, and then returns to the bucket to get more water. Each person in line turns and pours his or her cup into the cup of the next person in line. Play progresses down the line until the water gets to the last person, who runs to the bottle to pour it in. The first team to fill the bottle wins. The game sounds simple, but it gets challenging (and very silly and fun) when the cups start getting wet and flimsy.

Get It Right

Groups work together to finish a puzzle (word search, a crossword, or 50–100 piece jigsaw puzzle). Teams race to be the first team to complete the challenge.

SHARE AND CARE GROUPS

Checking in: Highs and lows of the week, prayer requests, and prayer

Warm up: Have you ever been so mad at another person that you swore you would never forgive him or her? How hard is it to forgive someone like Osama Bin Laden? Why? Have you ever turned your back on (and never forgiven) a friend who has wronged you in some way? Is there anything that person could do to earn your forgiveness?

FOCUS POINT

Video Option: In *Freaky Friday* (2003), the talk at the end of the movie between the mom and her daughter demonstrates forgiveness in a big way. (Start: 1:23:40; stop: 1:25:35.) Be sure to preview your selection. Remember you must have a video license. (<u>Video licensing information on CD</u>)

Archery Lesson Option: Have someone who is well-versed in the sport of archery come to demonstrate archery and speak with the youth. Let the youth each attempt to shoot an arrow at the target. (Note: If you know nothing about archery and don't know anyone who practices the sport, you can easily use a dart board, without the need for a guest.) As part of the demonstration, talk about the target being an image for Christians. The bull's-eye is the goal of Christlike living. Even when we are shooting toward the center, we frequently miss the mark. Each outer ring represents sins we commit. We have much for which to be forgiven.

- How hard was it for you to hold the bow?
- How close did your arrow come to the center of the target?
- Did you feel discouraged at your attempt to hit the center, or did you want to keep trying?
- What does this image say about our own lives? What can we learn?
- What are ways Christians practice getting closer to the mark? (*Going to church, Communion, Bible study, prayer, other traditional Christian practices*)

FOCUS THOUGHTS (Outline on CD)

Outline

Forgiveness comes hard for us. We want to hold on to grudges, pay people back, get revenge. Jesus shows us a better way to live.

1. **Our nature** seems to be to get back at people when they do something wrong to us. Letting go of the wrongs others have inflicted upon us is hard. We want to strike back, but that is not the model Jesus gave us for living. Jesus was on the cross; and his dying words were "Father, forgive them" (**Luke 23:34**).

2. **Our society** doesn't generally expect people to forgive one another. However, being a Christian often means that we go against what society says is OK; we have a higher standard. We are to forgive seventy-seven times, according to Jesus (**Matthew 18:22**). How many of you can keep track of forgiving seventy-seven times? Perhaps that's the point—not to keep score, but to be generous, as God has been generous in forgiving us.

3. **God forgives us.** Jesus died on the cross to take away the power of sin. He died to save our lives; and once forgiven, we are never the same. God's grace comes to us as a gift. When we accept the gift, our sins are forgiven and we can begin life fresh. We know that God has forgiven us and given us "second chances." So when we mess up and someone else offers us forgiveness and a second chance, we can humbly accept that gift also.

4. **Forgiving ourselves** is sometimes one of the hardest things we can do. For a variety of reasons, we often hold ourselves up to unreasonably high standards and spend our lives "beating ourselves up" for the wrongs we have committed. But God is there, consistently loving us and reminding us that we are God's own children. Yes, we will mess up, but God forgives; we too need to forgive ourselves and be blessed with the abundant life Jesus came to bring us. (**John 10:10**).

Let's pray.

Worship and Praise Music
- "Lose This Life," by Tait (*Lose This Life*)
- "Change," by Steven Curtis Chapman (*Speechless*)
- "Merciful Rain," by FHH (*City on a Hill*)

Create-a-Video

Create 30–60 second "commercials" about forgiveness. Record the performances with a video camera or just do them live! Let groups act out the commercials for one another during the closing or set up times in church services for them to perform.

Leader Scripture Exploration
- **Matthew 6:12-15** (Forgive us our debts)
- **Matthew 18:22** (We are to forgive beyond what we can keep track of.)
- **Luke 23:34** (Father, forgive them.)
- **Romans 6:1-14** (We are freed from sin.)
- **2 Corinthians 2:5-10** (Forgive and console the offender.)
- **Ephesians 4:31-32** (Put away bitterness and anger.)

Think About It

"I think that if God forgives us we must forgive ourselves."
— C.S. Lewis

(Additional quotations on CD)

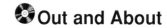Out and About

Go to a local cemetery. Initiate talk about how difficult it would be to lose someone who had wronged you (or vice versa) before reconciling with that person. Discuss the kind of impact that would have on your own life. Worship there.

(Additional idea on CD)

🔘 Service Project

Challenge each youth to reach out to someone with whom he or she needs to reconcile. It might be someone who has done something that a youth needs to forgive or it might be someone that he or she has wronged. Write notes of reconciliation and spend an afternoon delivering them. This project can become really fun if done together (there's strength in numbers!) Also, use some of the following tips for "packaging" the notes:

- Put the messages inside helium-filled balloons.

- Bake cupcakes. After baking, make a small hole from the bottom of the cupcake, place the note in the hole, frost the cupcake, and deliver!

(Additional ideas on CD)

🔘 Bumper Sticker

(Information on CD)

- Print out the bumper sticker found on the CD, and let the youth stand at the door of the sanctuary at the end of a service and hand them out. Or sell them for a quick and easy fundraiser.

🔘 Youth Witness Statement

- Invite a student to talk about the experience of forgiving or being forgiven. (How-to on CD)

🔘 FOCUS GROUP (Additional questions on CD)

Read aloud **John 21:15-19.**

Pass out a piece of play dough (or clay) for each person to mold as you talk. Give the group no instructions about what to do with it; just say, "Here is a piece of play dough for you." Then begin the discussion.

- Why does Jesus keep asking Peter if he loves him? *(Jesus' three questions echo Peter's three denials [John 13:37-38, 18:17, 25-27] and show his forgiveness.)*
- Why does he keep repeating what he wants Peter to do? *(Jesus is giving Peter a second chance.)*
- How easy or hard must it have been for Peter to accept the forgiveness and reconciliation that Jesus appeared to be offering?
- Have you ever been in a situation in which someone offered forgiveness to you but you were nervous or afraid to accept?
- Have you ever had that one special moment when you felt true forgiveness from another person? What did it feel like? Did it change the way you felt about what forgiveness really is?
- Have you ever offered that kind of forgiveness and reconciliation to someone else? How was it received?

At the end of the discussion, ask the youth to bring their play dough to the closing.

🔘 CLOSING

Remolded by Forgiveness

Set up an altar table with cans of play dough. As the youth enter, ask them to place their pieces of molded play dough or clay on the altar. Remind them that each piece looks different than it did when it was first purchased. They can no longer go back and make it look exactly the same as when it came out of the package, and yet it still is usable; it still has value. In many cases, it might even be prettier or more functional than it was at first.

Point out that this is also what sin does to us: It changes us and we can never go back to that original shape or dimension. And yet, through forgiveness and reconciliation, we can allow ourselves to become molded into something even better.

Invite the youth to take home a piece of the play dough or clay as a reminder that those moments of reconciliation create magnificent pieces of art!

Close with youth benediction (Numbers 6:24-26).

🔘 Prayer Path

Invite the youth to walk the path and to pray especially for the strength to reach out in reconciliation to the person with whom they need to offer forgiveness. (Prayer Path stations on CD)

PicTURe YOURSELF DeVOTeD

SOUL FOOD: Those times when we realize that other people's needs are more important than our own are moments of true humility and godliness.

SCRIPTURE: Ruth 1:1-16 (Ruth promises to follow Naomi.)

Games

I'm Stuck on You

One player is "It" for this fun tag game. It chases everyone until he or she tags a player. That player is then stuck to It, holding hands and becoming part of It. The growing It continues the game by chasing down another player. When the tenth player (or the last player if there are fewer than ten) is tagged, everyone is freed. The last player to join It becomes the new It, and the game continues.

Devotion Motion

This game is similar to Simon Says. Assign one person to be the caller. The other players are devoted to the caller (that is, they will hang on his or her every word). The caller will say something like, "I'm devoted to anyone who can do jumping jacks." Then all of the other youth must immediately do jumping jacks. If they don't do them, they're out. If the caller gives a direction without saying, "I'm devoted to anyone who can . . . ," prior to the directions and someone does the action, he or she is out.

SHARE AND CARE GROUPS

Checking in: Highs and lows of the week, prayer requests, and prayer

Warm up: Ask the youth, "Are you a better leader or follower?" Ask the youth to give some examples to support their answers. Ask, "What does the word *devoted* mean to you? What are you devoted to?"

Have IT YOUR WAY!
Choose from, adapt, or rearrange these elements to create the best soul feast for your youth group.

THE FIXiN'S
More fun stuff to make the theme extra special! Your choice.

Munchies

For snacks that enhance this particular learning, it's not so much the food they eat as they way they eat it that counts!

• Serving Souls: Have youth pair up and tie the left hand of one to the right hand of the other. Then tell each pair to go through the snack line, making a snack for each of them (something that requires teamwork like peanut butter and jelly sandwiches or ice cream sundaes), then go to the table and eat. They will soon learn that teamwork is the most important ingredient in this recipe!

• Chocolate Fondue (Recipe and discussion questions on CD) Follow a similar plan as with Serving Souls (above).

Heart-shaped cookies or candy hearts are also good munchies for the theme of being devoted.

Popular Songs

Use these before and/or after the program to engage the youth. These are some options. Try to include the latest appropriate popular songs.

• "Hopelessly Devoted to You," by Olivia Newton-John (*Grease: The Original Soundtrack From the Motion Picture*)
• "Anywhere for You," by Backstreet Boys (*Backstreet Boys*)
• "Devotion," by Earth, Wind, and Fire (*Open Our Eyes*)
• "Stuck on You," by Lionel Richie (*Can't Slow Down*)
• "You're My Best Friend," by Queen (*Greatest Hits*)
• "I Just Called to Say I Love You," by Stevie Wonder (*Song Review— A Greatest Hits Collection*)

Worship and Praise Music

• "I Could Sing of Your Love Forever," by SonicFlood (*I Could Sing of Your Love Forever*)
• "Lord, I Lift Your Name on High," by SonicFlood (*I Could Sing of Your Love Forever*)
• "Above All," by Rebecca Saint James (*I Could Sing of Your Love Forever*)

Out and About

• Visit the newborn ward of your local hospital. Take a few minutes to observe the care and devotion the newborns receive in that room. Talk about the love and care you experience as a child of God. Or visit with a family from your church who have an infant.

• Go to a senior adult center to visit with the residents. Again observe the devotion paid to each. Have your worship time in a multi-function room at the center. Invite the senior adults to join you.

Focus Point

Video Option: *Pay It Forward* (2000) is filled with many glimpses of devotion, but an especially good one illustrates devotion in several ways—devotion to an idea and devotion of people to each other. (Start: 1:51:24; stop 1:57:48.) Be sure to preview your selection to avoid any content that would be objectionable in your setting. Remember that you must have a video license. (Video licensing information on CD)

Activity Option: Trust Me! Use this activity and the debriefing questions with it to explore the concept of following someone blindly. This trust experience demands that a youth totally trust another youth to be his or her leader. (Instructions and questions on CD)

Focus Thoughts (Outline on CD)

Outline

In our everyday relationships, we can be very loyal individuals. We are willing to follow our friends to the end of the earth, or so we think. Yet when the relationships are damaged or severed, the last thing we want to do is continue hanging around. That's one of the things that makes this story of Ruth and Naomi so powerful. Ruth is willing to trade her secure past for an unknown future. Few of us would have the guts to do that.

Key Points:

1. Naomi and her husband, Elimelech, left Bethlehem because of the famine there and went to live in a land called Moab. While in Moab, their two sons married Moabite women. Within about ten years, the father and the two sons had died, leaving all three women without husbands. In that time, becoming a widow was not only emotionally but also economically devastating. Widows had no means of support.

2. Naomi heard that the famine was coming to an end in her homeland and so prepared to return to Bethlehem. As she started on the journey home, she told both daughters-in-law to return to their own families, where they would have hope of being cared for.

3. One of them, Orpah, left and went home; the other, Ruth, vowed to stay with Naomi and make Naomi's home her home. She also chose to make Naomi's God her God.

4. The selflessness that Ruth felt for Naomi was something that many of us have never experienced. How many of us would really give up our own biological families to spend the rest of our lives with our in-laws? Ruth saw Naomi's need and was willing to put it before her own.

5. We can experience moments of selflessness by focusing on what other people need, instead of what we ourselves need or want.

FOCUS GROUP (Additional questions on CD)

Read aloud **Ruth 1:1-16.**

- What do you think Ruth meant by "your people shall be my people, and your God my God"?
- Have you ever felt that kind of devotion to someone?
- Hand out index cards or pieces of paper and pens. Have the youth draw a face to indicate what they think Naomi was feeling when Ruth insisted that she go with her. Have youth volunteer to show the rest of the group the face they drew and talk about why they chose the particular emotion. Then have the youth turn the card or paper over and draw a face to represent what they think Ruth was feeling. Again, let volunteers Do "show and tell" around the group again.
- Have you ever had one of those "ah-ha" moments when you realized just how much someone else loves you? What did it feel like? How did it affect how you acted toward that person from that point on?
- What are some ways that you, as a Christian, devote yourself to the needs of others? How have those persons been helped? How have you been helped because of your devotion?

CLOSING

The Devotion Habit (Devotional resources on CD)

Throughout the ages, Christians have practiced the spiritual discipline of "doing devotions." Usually, the devotions are a prayer and a brief reading, often with a Scripture. Many Christian individuals have daily devotions; others experience the practice when they gather with fellow Christians. The point of doing devotions is to show love to God; and in doing those things that bring us closer to God, we are also drawn closer to one another. Conversely, when we do those things that show selfless devotion to the needs of others, we are brought closer to God.

To illustrate this relationship, have a group of six to ten persons stand in a circle. (If the whole group is very large, they may either watch a representative group or break into smaller groups to do this.) Have this small group stand about an arm's length from one another. Tell them to imagine that at the center of the circle is God. Have the group move closer to God. What happens? (*They also move closer to one another.*) If they draw nearer to one another, they will also draw nearer to God.

Invite the youth to begin a habit of personal devotions so that they will grow closer to God. Close with prayer.

Prayer Path

Close with the Prayer Path, or remind the youth of the times during the week that it will be available for them. (Prayer Path stations on CD)

Ah-ha Moments Celebration

(Instructions on CD)

Service Projects

Givin' It Up: Ask the youth to give up one weekend to devote to meeting the needs of people in your community. Ideas to consider are:

- Painting a room or two of your church or community center
- Repairing and re-painting playground equipment at the local elementary school or daycare
- Planting a garden for a nursing home or assisted living center
- Planning and implementing a one-day carnival in your town (have games, crafts, story-time,—be creative with activities)
- Play board games, cards, shuffleboard, and so forth at the local senior adult center

(Additional ideas on CD)

Think About It

"Identify your highest skill and devote your time to performing it."
—*God's Little Instruction Book for Leaders* (Honor Books: 1997, page 240)

Framed!

Take individual photos of each youth. Create picture frames by copying the graphic (Design on CD) on to magnetic sheets (available at computer supply stores) and cutting them out. Have each youth take the framed pictures to school and hang them inside their lockers as a daily reminder to stay devoted to Jesus.

GOD LOVES GOOD SEX

GOD CREATED SEX

Many of us forget that God created sex. That fact means we should look to God as the authority on how sex should be a part of our life. It also means that sex is a good thing (when used the way God intended). Do you want good sex? Listen to the truth about sex from the One who invented it in the first place.

APPETIZERS (Additional ideas on CD)

Publicity Ideas: *Youth get persistent messages from media and society about sex. Be as persistent in getting out God's message about sex! Use these ideas and others of your own.*

- **Sweeten the deal**. Put together small bags of Hershey's Kisses and Hugs. Add a note inviting your youth to the programs.

- **Mail postcards:** Create postcards using either the theme logo (<u>Logo on CD</u>) or the poster (<u>Design on CD</u>). Mail these to the youth a week or two before the program. Include the time, dates, and location.

- **Inform parents.** One to two weeks before the program, send via e-mail or in a letter the research material (<u>"Parents—You Really Count!" on CD</u>) along with a message informing the parents of the program series and why you think it's important for their son or daughter to attend. Offer to meet with any parents who have questions or who wish to know more about the series. According to research, parents have significant influence in teens' decisions about sexual activity. Empower them. Encourage them to begin conversations with their sons and daughters.

- **Invite other adults.** You should never try to do a program alone with a group of youth, but having additional adults is especially important when discussing a topic such as sex. Invite some key adults in your congregation to sit in on the program. They need not be parents of your youth. In fact, it might be best if they were not, since you will want the youth to feel free to talk during discussion times.

- **Give out coupons.** If you choose to videotape random, on-the-street interviews, make sure that you have cards to hand out to those you interview. The cards should say something such as "Want to see yourself onscreen? Come to . . . (*insert location, date, and time*). Present this card for a free (*insert whatever item or service you will give as an incentive to come*)."

COMBOS MENU

Main Dishes

Weekly Program Options: *Choose one or all; do in any order. Check each description for variations and the fixin's. Invite a team of youth to plan with you.*

1. **Sex in the World Today**—It's everywhere! Media and pop culture constantly push sex. But it comes with a hook: buy! buy! buy! God, who has the best possible life for you in mind, cares for your well being and for the truth. Media and culture care about keeping the customer interested and buying. Which will you believe?

2. **God Tells You Why**—God has drawn tight lines in relation to sex, letting us know what is good and what is not. But there are good reasons for the boundaries! Find out why.

3. **How Far Is Too Far?**—If we're going to be in an intimate relationship with someone, then we can't help but wonder how intimate is too intimate. Does God draw a line? Should I draw a line? How do I know where the line should be? How do I stop myself from going over the line?

4. **Starting All Over**—OK, so you've messed up. Most people do in one way or another. Or you may wonder what happens if you do go too far. *Will God still love me?* Find out how God makes things whole again. In Christ, all things are made new—including you.

Spice It Up

Theme Decorations: *With this topic, be sure to talk with your pastor and others in authority to let them know what you are studying and why these pictures are a part of that. NOTE: If your space is used during the week for other meetings, you may avoid some problems by taking down the pictures between meetings.*

- Decorate your walls with advertisements that use sexual imagery to sell items that are unrelated to sexuality.

- Use posters and items from the office of an OB/GYN, such as pictures of the growth of a baby during gestation, diseases, and basic sex-ed diagrams. Turn your meeting room into a doctor's office. In fact, if you can bring in a doctor for the sessions, he or she may be able to help with any tough questions you might not be able to answer.

- Supply a question box. Have a box available where youth can place anonymous questions. Hand out cards to the youth, and invite them to write questions or comments on the cards. Tell the youth that you will try to address each question you receive during these or future programs.

- If you have a commitment service as part of the program (see pages 50 and 53), use candelabras, banners, paraments, and other items your church makes available for weddings.

SEX IN THE WORLD TODAY

Have It Your Way!

Choose from, adapt, or rearrange these elements to create the best soul feast for your youth group.

The Fixin's

More fun stuff to make the theme extra special! Your choice.

Munchies

Provide candy hearts with messages or Sweetarts.

Popular Songs

Use these before and/or after the program to engage the youth. These are some options. Try to include the latest appropriate popular songs.

- "Don't Stand So Close to Me," by The Police (*Every Breath You Take: The Classics*)
- "Roxanne," by The Police (*Every Breath You Take: The Classics*)
- "Who Wrote the Book of Love?" by The Monotones (*Who Wrote the Book of Love?*)
- "Everyday I Write the Book," by Elvis Costello (*The Very Best of Elvis Costello and the Attractions*)
- "Love Shack," by B-52's (*Cosmic Thing*)
- "Irene," by TobyMac (*Momentum*)
- "Lonely People," by Jars of Clay (*Who We Are Instead*) or America (*The Complete Greatest Hits*)

Worship and Praise Music

- "Agnus Dei," by Michael W. Smith (*Worship*) or Third Day (*Offering: A Worship Album*)
- "More Love, More Power," Michael W. Smith (*Worship*)
- "Above All," Michael W. Smith (*Worship*)

SOUL FOOD: God loves good sex, but you won't find good sex by listening to what the world says!

SCRIPTURE: Matthew 7:15-20 (You will know the good and the bad, the wolves, by their fruit.)

 **Games** (Additional game on CD)

Touch

Have everyone in the group line up in a particular order (alphabetical, by height, by age). The leader shouts an object that everyone can see. All the players run and touch that object and then get back into their place in line. The last person to return to his or her place sits out.

The Great Race

Put together teams of up to five persons. Have two youth volunteer to be partners. The one person grabs the waist or jumps on the back of the other person (who is blindfolded). The one being carried runs the blindfolded partner through an obstacle course by giving directions. The rest of the team forms the cheering squad. Compete by timing each pair. Give prizes for best time, for the funniest pair, for persistence, for the loudest-cheering team!

SHARE AND CARE GROUPS

Checking in: Highs and lows of the week, prayer requests, and prayer

Warm up: Pass a package wrapped and all decorated with ribbon around the group, inviting them each to shake it and try to guess what's inside. As they're passing it among the group, ask if anyone in the group has trouble waiting to open gifts. Ask which is more difficult: knowing what a gift is and not being able to use it or not knowing what it is until the time to use it?

FOCUS POINT

Video Option: In the week prior to this program, record commercials that use sex as a lure to "hook" consumers. Or, record various sitcoms and the way they use sex to draw an audience. Or, record some sections of popular music videos that use sex to sell the music.

Music Option: Play Janet Jackson's song "Damita Jo" (*Damita Jo* [clean version]). Have the lyrics available for youth to read during the playing of the song.

FOCUS THOUGHTS (Text on CD)

Let me tell you about a man who was one of God's beloved followers. The Bible tells us that this man was chosen by God to lead God's people. In fact, God told this man that the salvation of the world would come through his offspring.

No matter how holy and chosen this man was, though, he experienced sexual temptation. He ultimately made choices based on lust—not love—that had terrible consequences. Sex, used in ways other than God intended, has the power to disrupt lives and mess up the future—even for the most focused followers of God. That's what happened to David.

Accidentally, at first, David saw something he shouldn't have—a woman bathing. Watching her soon became no longer accidental. Lust overtook his heart. He had her brought to his home. He used his charm (and the fact that he was the woman's king) to seduce her. When she became pregnant, he called her husband home from battle to cover up his own role in the pregnancy. But her husband followed a soldier's code of honor and would not have sex with his wife or enjoy the other pleasures of life while his men were fighting for their lives. Desperate to hide the sin, David sent the faithful soldier back into battle with secret orders that he be placed on the front lines, where he was indeed killed. David married the woman. God's spokesperson confronted David with the sin; and consequently, when the baby was born, David's child died.

Lives were changed. Love was destroyed. Sex is powerful.

You know that sex is powerful. You've experienced its power in your own home as you turn on the TV or as you open a fashion magazine. The media use sex to hook your attention and make you remember and buy what it is they are trying to sell. The writers for the TV show know that sex will get you to tune in again next time; and the more popular the show, the more dollars they rake in. The music industry knows that if you are drawn by sex in their music video, then you're more likely to buy that CD or to ask to see that video again and again. The media promote the idea that sex outside of marriage is OK, expected, and even helpful to a relationship.

These examples abuse God's gift of sex. They are ways of using sex for something other than what God intended. God intended sex to strengthen bonds of love in a committed, marriage relationship. What the world mostly shows us about sex, though, is lies. Our culture pushes you to open this package of sex too soon, rather than to wait on the timing instructed by God, the giver of that gift in the first place.

The media don't tell you some things about sex that are truths that you should know. For example, research by the University of Chicago concluded that married sex is, in fact, the type of sex that satisfies people the most. Married people with only one life partner (that is, people who are married who only have had sex with the person with whom they are married) are most likely to report they are extremely or very satisfied with the amount of physical and emotional pleasure they experience in their sex lives.

Too many corporations and marketing people don't want to tell you the truth about sex. They want to use sex for a lure and hook you. They want you to believe that having sex before marriage is no big thing, that it's OK, and

Other Movie Options

Choose one of these movies, or ask students to recommend a more recent release. Be sure to preview your selection to avoid any content that would be objectionable in your setting. Remember that you must have a video license.
(Video licensing information on CD)

• *The End of the Affair* (R) (1999)
• *Pleasantville* (1998)
• *Almost Famous* (2000)
• *Forrest Gump* (1994)

On-the-Street Interviews

Have the youth videotape random youth at the mall (or random church members at various church functions); ask this question: What is your favorite thing that God created?

Leader Scripture Exploration

• **2 Samuel 11:1–12:23** (David's sin)
• **Romans 7:15-24** (Inner conflict)

On Screen

Key points of presentation
(PowerPoint® on CD)

Out and About

Make plans for your group to meet at the office of an OB/GYN or in the waiting room on a maternity ward. Invite the doctor to sit in on the program and even to offer a question and answer time.

💿 Youth Witness Statement

Try to find a youth or two (or college-age person) in your church who will talk candidly with the students about the struggles to stay away from sexual temptation. They could make this humorous, but the talk should point out the frustration and barrage of sexual content and images that are focused on teenagers and young adults today.
(How-to on CD)

Invite Commitment

Ask your youth to make a commitment to come to the next three sessions and to bring an open mind. Tell them a part of this commitment is so they can determine the truth. Make a commitment to them that you will be up front and honest with them in dealing with this issue.

even necessary if the relationship is going to work. These people want you to believe that everyone is doing it and that you cannot be hurt by it.

Such advice reminds me of Jesus' warning to his disciples about wolves in sheep's clothing. In **Matthew 7:15-17** Jesus says,

> "Beware of false prophets, who come to you in sheep's clothing but inwardly are ravenous wolves. You will know them by their fruits. Are grapes gathered from thorns, or figs from thistles? In the same way, every good tree bears good fruit, but the bad tree bears bad fruit."

Those who try to sell you the line about sex being available and OK for you when you are not married are not interested in your well being. Take a look at who it is that pushes this thinking—the media and business corporations, who have dollars to gain by getting you involved in sex. Their dollars come at your expense! God, on the other hand, has your best in mind.

God wants you to have good sex (after all, God created sex). God wants you to use this gift that God has created in the best way possible—in a committed marriage relationship with your spouse. Now, you have to decide whom you can trust. Are you going to believe the media and our society who push their idea of good sex in order to get you to tune in and buy? Or are you going to believe God, who created you, who created sex, and who wants only the best for you—always? Let's pray.

FOCUS GROUP

- What do you think about the statement that married sex is actually the type of sex that satisfies people the most? Why do you think that is the case?
- According to a study by the National Survey of Family Growth, (USA) women who have premarital sex increase their odds of divorce by about 60 percent. Why do you suppose culture seems to tell us the opposite—that having sex with someone before you marry them is a great way to help the relationship?
- Why do you think God would create you with sexual urges and desires as a teenager but still want you to wait until marriage to enjoy sex?
- What are some ways a teenager can have control in the struggle between physical desire and what's right?

CLOSING

The Gift

Use the wrapped gift box from the warm up (page 42). Hold it out for all to see; place it on the altar. Talk briefly based on these points:

- The gift box is symbolic of the good gift of sexuality God has given to us.
- *At the right time*, the unwrapping is very special. That's not society's message, but it is God's.
- We have to decide in whom we will place our trust.

Close with prayer or individual prayer time at the altar.

GOD TELLS YOU WHY

SOUL FOOD: Sex within a committed marriage relationship brings good to both partners; sex outside of marriage has great potential for harm.

SCRIPTURE: 1 Corinthians 6:18-20 (Don't be immoral in matters of sex. That is a sin against your body, which is the temple of the Holy Spirit.)

Games (Additional game on CD)

Body Part Shuffle

Partners stand facing each other in one large double circle. One player, "It," stands in the center and calls "Face to face," "Back to back," "Knees to knees." The players taking their positions accordingly. When It calls "Change," all players find new partners. It tries to get a partner, too. If It finds a new partner, then the player who is left alone becomes the new It, moves to the center and begins giving commands. The calls may be varied with "Elbows to elbows," "Left foot to left foot," "Nose to nose," and so on.

Long-Lost Love

Players are seated in a circle with one player blindfolded in the center. The blindfolded player moves around the circle to a seated player, drops to one knee and says to the one seated, "Are you my long-lost love?" The seated player must answer in some sort of disguised voice. He or she may bark, chirp, meow, groan, or answer in any vocal way he or she wishes. The blindfolded player is allowed one guess to name the seated person. If the guess is correct, then the seated person must become the blindfolded person. If the guess is incorrect, then the blindfolded person must find another seated person and begin the question again.

SHARE AND CARE GROUPS

Checking in: Highs and lows of the week, prayer requests, and prayer

Warm up: Have the youth make a list of "Things the World Tells Us About Sex," using such headings as, "Sex Outside of Marriage," "Talking Trash" (how we talk about sex), "Having a Fantasy-Filled Life" (pornography or lust). Have them brainstorm messages they get in these areas. (Examples: It's OK to live together before married if you really "love" each other; other sexual contact is OK in dating as long as you don't go "all the way"; It's OK to visit porn sites on the Internet; after all, it's not hurting anybody.)

HAVE IT YOUR WAY!

Choose from, adapt, or rearrange these elements to create the best soul feast for your youth group.

THE FIXIN'S

More fun stuff to make the theme extra special! Your choice.

Munchies

Serve jelly-filled donuts or tacos. Point out that when the "boundaries" (taco shell or donut) are broken, the stuff inside spills out and makes a mess.

Popular Songs

Use these before and/or after the program to engage the youth. These are some options. Try to include the latest appropriate popular songs.

- "Who Wrote the Book of Love?" by the Monotones (*Who Wrote the Book of Love?*)
- "Free Man," by Angie Aparo (*The American*)
- "Chapel of Love," by The Dixie Cups (*The Very Best of the Dixie Cups: Chapel of Love*)
- "Close to You," by The Carpenters (*Gold: 35th Anniversary Edition*)

Worship and Praise Music

- "Thy Word," by Amy Grant (*Collection*)
- "Step by Step," by Rich Mullins (*Songs 2*)
- "Word of God Speak," by MercyMe (*Spoken For*)

Other Movie Options

Choose one of these movies, or ask students to recommend a more recent release. Be sure to preview your selection to avoid any content that would be objectionable in your setting. Remember that you must have a video license.
(Video licensing information on CD)

• *The Confession* (R) (1999)
• *The Devil's Advocate* (R) (1997)
• *The Truman Show* (1998)
• *Face/Off* (R) (1997) (dealing with how temptation and wrong choices often masquerade as something good or right)

Leader Exploration Scripture

1 Thessalonians 4:1-8 (Living to please God)

On Screen

(PowerPoint® on CD)

On-the-Street Interviews

Have the youth videotape random youth at the mall (or random church members at various church functions); ask this question: What are some rules from God that are difficult for you or people you know to follow?

Focus Point

Video Options: *Cider House Rules* (1999) When someone who can read finally reads the rules for them, the laborers laugh at the rules that are posted in the bunkhouse. They have broken every one and will continue to do so. One of the characters says that those rules don't pertain to them because they didn't make the rules and they can't even read them. They have their own ideas about what's right and wrong. (Start 1:43; stop 1:45. Times are approximate.)

Skit Option: Work with a team of youth to come up with and present a brief skit that illustrates one or more of the scenarios suggested by the Focus Thoughts. Present the skit(s) before the Focus Thoughts or at the appropriate time in the talk itself. (Ideas on CD)

Focus Thoughts (Text on CD)

The culture today is saturated by sex. Turn on a TV show and you see people living together. It's treated as no big deal. You listen to music and hear the singer fantasize about a girl he sees; you watch a music video or simply turn a page in a magazine and you see images that are close to pornography; you log onto the Internet and get spam e-mail offering some sort of sexual gratification if you'll visit a particular website. What the makers of these images and messages want you to believe is that all this is normal and expected.

But God is saying something different. If you're unsure about what to believe, just look at the motivation behind the message. The marketers want you to believe what they're pushing, because it sells the product. God wants you to believe what God says because God cares for you.

Read aloud **1 Corinthians 6:18-20** (*preferably in the Contemporary English Version*).

God has one basic rule about sex: Sex is for a committed marriage relationship. That means no adultery (or sex with someone other than the person to whom you are married), no premarital sex (even if you plan to marry each other), and no casual sex (the kind that is promoted as just for "fun"). Why would God draw such tight lines?

Because God wants the best for you. You and others can so easily get hurt—big time—if you cross the lines. For example:

• What happens when a husband or wife has an affair? Broken trust, perhaps broken marriage. What if they have children and the marriage breaks up? Who gets hurt? For how long? What happens if the person outside the marriage eventually is cut loose? How does he or she feel? Where is trust? Where is happiness? What if that person is also married? perhaps has children?

• What happens when a dating couple have sex? Do they take the time and effort to truly know each other, or does the desire for sex blind them to who each of them is as a whole person? What if one person thinks that having sex is the same as being loved; but to the other, having sex is just having sex? When the novelty wears off, one leaves and the other feels used and discarded. What if sex results in a pregnancy, but the baby isn't wanted? Or the mother (most often) has to take on the enormous task of providing for the child and being a parent all alone? What happens to the mother's plans for her future?

- What happens when sex is casual, including viewing pornography on the Internet? The individuals are simply using the other person. There is no caring about the other, no respect for the other. Sex is all about "me." What if one person has a sexually transmitted disease, would he or she care enough about the other person to not have sex? Not likely. How would a person begin to feel about himself or herself if sex never came with love?

Do you know what a sexual ghost is? A sexual ghost is a memory that a person has of a past sexual experience with someone. Here's an example: A young man has sex with a girl whom he thinks he loves. For some reason or another that relationship ends, and he no longer plans on marrying that person. Years later this guy does, in fact, fall in love and marry someone else. He's sure of this lady. They're meant for each other. They are in love. The problem is there's this memory—this ghost—living in the couple's bedroom. Every time they begin to get intimate there is a third person there with them—the memory of that first sexual experience. It haunts their love life. It haunts their sex life. Whether that first time was positive or negative, it will always be a memory and a comparison to the man's married sex. God has forgiven him. His wife has forgiven him. Maybe even this man has forgiven himself, but that doesn't stop the consequences of the decision. Having sex before marriage is always a big deal because it has lasting consequences.

God wants something better for you. The God of love wants you to experience love that values you as a whole person, that supports and encourages you, and that calls you out of any self-centeredness to discover the joy of loving others. In a committed marriage relationship partners focus on building up each other, building up their children, and ultimately building up their community. Because they have experienced love, they in turn can bring love to others.

That's what God wants for you. Don't settle for less. Let's pray.

 **FoCUS GRoUP** (Alternative questions on CD)

- Work together to make a list of what values and attitudes are a part of a loving, committed, marriage relationship. How would the partners treat each other?
- Do you think sex is good because the quality of the relationship is good, or is the quality of the relationship good because the sex is good?

 **CLoSING**

Psalm 119 Litany (Handout on CD)

Make a Commitment (Handout on CD)

Ask the youth to make a commitment to pray for God's guidance as they learn about God's Word on sex and deal with their own struggles with sexual temptation. Hand out copies of the sample prayer.

From the Trenches

Try to find an adult in your church who will candidly talk about his or her experiences with sex before marriage. Perhaps you have an unwed parent who was never married or an adult who had decided to "move in" with a past girlfriend (or boyfriend) rather then get married. This individual should talk about the feelings and consequences that occurred from such a decision.

Out and About

Make plans for your group to meet at the courthouse and then at the altar in the church. At both places talk about the legitimacy of marriage and the similarities as well as the differences between the state recognition of marriage and a marriage before God.

Youth Witness Statement

Ask a youth or two (or college-age person) in your church to talk candidly with the students about what helps him or her follow God's word—things like an active prayer life, study of Scripture, having an accountability partner, being active in a Christian community. (How-to on CD)

HOW FAR IS TOO FAR?

Have It Your Way!
Choose from, adapt, or rearrange these elements to create the best soul feast for your youth group.

The Fixin's
More fun stuff to make the theme extra special! Your choice.

Munchies
Set out bowls of Hershey's Kisses and Hugs.

Popular Songs
Use these before and/or after the program to engage the youth. These are some options. Try to include the latest appropriate popular songs.

- "Point of 'Know' Return," by Kansas (*Sail On: The 30th Anniversary Collection 1974–2004*)
- "How Deep Is Your Love?" by The BeeGees (*Their Greatest Hits: The Record*)

Worship and Praise Music
- "Trading My Sorrows," by Darrell Evans (*Freedom*)
- "Open the Eyes of My Heart," by Paul Baloche (*Open the Eyes of My Heart*)
- "Every Move I Make," by David Ruis (*Every Move I Make*)

SOUL FOOD: Thinking through boundaries ahead of time keeps us from crossing a line and being hurt.

SCRIPTURE: 2 Timothy 2:22 (Shun what is hurtful; run after righteousness, faith, love, and peace; choose to be with people who love the Lord.)

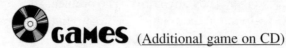

Games (Additional game on CD)

Elbow Tag
Pairs link arms and stand scattered around the room. A chaser and a runner weave among the pairs. The runner can switch with anyone by linking arms with either player of a pair. The other player of the pair becomes the runner and must leave at once. If the runner is tagged by the chaser, he or she becomes the chaser. The game is more fun if runners link arms often.

Shoe Pile
Have pairs move to the outside walls of the room. Hand out a blindfold to each pair. One person of each pair puts on the blindfold. The players without blindfolds remove their shoes and put them all in a pile in the center of the room. When you say, "go," the blindfolded partner must go to the pile of shoes and find each shoe of his or her partner. Partners may call out instructions but only from their position against the wall. When the searchers find the shoes, they must put them on the feet of partners (and tie them if they can be tied) before removing their blindfolds.

SHARE AND CARE GROUPS

Checking in: Highs and lows of the week, prayer requests, and prayer

Warm up: Place a line of tape on the floor (or draw a line with chalk or in the dirt if outside). Line the group up at the far end of the room and tell them that when you say, "go," they should run toward the line and stop as close to the line as possible without going over. Do the exercise only once, asking the youth to stay where they ended.

Ask: Why did you go over the line? Why were you able to stop from going over the line? Where did you begin to slow down? Why? If the line were actually the edge of the Grand Canyon, how would you have approached it?

FOCUS Point

Video Option: *A Walk to Remember*. Landon brings the blanket to the star-watching date. The two briefly discuss being seduced but go in a healthful way.

Music Option: "Paradise by the Dashboard Light," by Meatloaf (*The Very Best of Meatloaf*)

FOCUS Thoughts (Text and handouts on CD)

This question of "How far is too far?" is a question that many ask when they're dating. We want to know how far we can go physically in a relationship and still be "OK." Where does God say, "Not beyond this point"?

But asking a question like that reminds me of the analogy of dating and baseball. Each generation has its own rules of how far you can go on a first date or a third date or after you've been dating for a month. Each generation has its own definition of "first base" and "second base."

When we draw a line and say, "Do anything you want up to this line" we tend to invite people to get as close to that line as they can. I remember riding in the car with my sister when we were kids. Whenever we got into an argument, we'd end up drawing an imaginary line down the center of the back seat; we had this rule that we had to stay on our own half. We couldn't cross the line. I was really good at getting close, though. I'd get right up to the edge—not because I necessarily needed all that room. I just wanted to see how close I could get.

The problem was that sometimes the car would hit a bump, or dad would go around a corner and one of us would slide over the line we had drawn. We weren't always ready for the unexpected; and because we had played so close to the edge of the line, we were that much more likely to go over it when forces beyond our control came into the picture.

Think about the experiment we did in our Share and Care groups. Many of you discovered the power of momentum. It was hard to stop where you wanted to once you got going, unless you slowed down well before the mark. That's a good image to keep in mind. Human sexuality has a momentum of its own, which can be hard to stop at appropriate points if we play too close to the line.

Sexual intimacy changes a relationship. In the context of a committed marriage relationship, the change is good. It deepens the bonds of love. But without the context of commitment that marriage brings, sexual intimacy has great potential for someone getting badly hurt.

I know that many people say, "Well, God is against premarital intercourse. I'll draw the line at intercourse; but it's OK to do other sexual things, like oral sex." No, whenever genitals are involved, you're playing too close to the line. Someone will get hurt. That level of intimacy is meant for marriage.

When I was dating the woman who is now my wife, at the point that I was pretty sure that we had a good thing going and that I wanted our relationship to continue growing, I told her that I didn't want to mess it up. I said that I was very attracted to her; but that, because of my own beliefs and for the sake of our relationship, I did not want us to have any kind of sex. We talked about it, and we agreed that any physical part of our relationship would not go in that direction.

Other Movie Options

Note: Because of the topic of sex, many movie possibilities may have some scenes that are inappropriate for viewing. There are some scenes within these suggestions, however, that, if viewed and chosen ahead, are appropriate and can be helpful in the program.

Choose one or more of the movies listed, or ask students to recommend a more recent release. Be sure to preview your selection to avoid any content that would be objectionable in your setting. Remember that you must have a video license. (Video licensing information on CD)

* *Changing Lanes*
* *Thelma and Louise* (final scene where they drive over the cliff)
* *Cool Hand Luke* (1967) Luke reacts differently than the rest of the prisoners when an attractive woman washes her car.

Talk Tip

Cue two volunteers to act out the brother and sister scene as you talk: fighting and drawing their imaginary line; then the bump or the curve!

Leader Scripture Exploration

* **Genesis 2:15-17** and **Genesis 3:1-3**. What are the differences in the two "boundaries"? Why might Adam or Eve have added the additional boundary of touching the fruit?
* **Matthew 5:27-28** (Degrees of sin)

On Screen

Key points of presentation (PowerPoint® on CD)

On-the-Street Interviews

Have the youth videotape random youth at the mall (or random church members at various church functions); ask this question: What do you think are the "bases" in dating for kids these days (first base, second base, third base, home run)?

Out and About

Take the group to a baseball diamond and have your program there. Do the closing at the pitcher's mound, since God is the one who "pitches" the gift of sex to us.

Youth Witness Statement

Ask a youth or two (or college-age person) in your church to talk candidly with the students about a time when he or she "crossed the line." The talks should focus on consequences and the need for pre-determined boundaries. (How-to on CD)

Poster

Good sex—It's not about rounding the bases! (Design on CD)

Token

Give each person some sort of ring or wristband—an actual metal band, fishing line with beads, or perhaps a small strip of leather or cloth that can be tied around the finger or wrist.

That discussion *helped* our relationship in a lot of ways. It meant that neither one of us had to wonder whether the other one wanted to go farther. It gave us each permission to keep the other one accountable. And it acknowledged that we were very attracted to each other but were more interested in the long-term relationship than in a desire of the moment. We figured out our boundaries, and we helped each other stick to them. We grew closer in other ways because we had dealt with the issue. (*Like the video scene in* Walk to Remember.)

So how far is too far? What boundaries should you set? Here are a few things that will help you figure out your boundaries: (*These are both on the PowerPoint® and in the CD as a handout.*)

- Decide why you're in this relationship. If it's all about you—what you get and what you want—then it's not right.
- Ask yourself whether your relationship is hindering or helping your (and your girlfriend's or boyfriend's) relationship with God. If it's bringing you or the other one down, then something's not right.
- Draw your personal line back a ways from where you think God wants you to go. Don't try to get as close to God's line as you can. Respect momentum.
- Figure out how far you will allow yourself go before you're on that date—not "how far *can* I get" (that smacks of a "me" focus and lack of respect for the other person). It's a lot easier to put on the brakes when you've already decided where you will stop.
- Talk about the physical aspect of your relationship up front with your boyfriend or girlfriend. Let him or her know your feelings and where the line is so that he or she can help keep your relationship healthy and not hurtful. This talk also helps the other person know that you're not expecting him or her to go farther. (You'll earn lots of respect for that one.)

Today's Scripture from **2 Timothy 2:22** tells us to shun what is hurtful, but to run after righteousness, faith, love, and peace. It also encourages us to choose to be with people who love the Lord. Let these three things help you set healthy, loving boundaries in your relationships. Let's pray.

FOCUS GROUP

- Why do we want to know boundaries? How are they helpful?
- What boundaries help you? What boundaries hurt you?
- How does choosing to be with people who love the Lord help us deal with sexual temptation? How helpful are your friends in these matters?

CLOSING

Psalm 40 Litany (Handout on CD)

Make a Commitment (Additional ideas on CD)

Invite the youth to make a commitment to sexual abstinence until they are married. Do it simply, extending the invitation and giving a token ring or wristband. Or create a more elaborate ceremony, placing the commitment in the context of a wedding and worship.

Starting Over

S⊙UI F⊙⊙D: Any of us can mess up, but through the grace of God, we can start over. We don't have to live with guilt.

SCRiPTURE: Psalm 32:3, 5 (When I refused to confess my sin, I was miserable....Finally, I confessed my sin, God forgave me! All my guilt is gone.)

 ## Games (Additional game on CD)

Fan the Hearts

Beforehand, cut paper hearts from tissue paper (the kind used in wrapping gifts). You may cut them in layers, but you need to separate them before distributing. Divide into groups of five to seven. Each group forms a circle. In the center of each circle, put a large aluminum pie tin on the floor. Sprinkle tissue paper hearts around the tins. Give each player a paper plate to be used as a fan. At a signal, everyone fans with the plate, trying to blow the hearts into the pie tins. The harder the fanning, the higher the hearts fly. The team with the most hearts in the pan after the allotted time (3–5 minutes) wins.

Group Up

A leader stands at the center of the room with a large pot and a metal spoon (anything loud and with a unique sound can be used). Instructions are given that the youth are to gather into groups numbering the same as the number of hits on the pot. For example: if the leader hits the pot four times, then youth must get into groups of four. Once all of the groups are formed, the leader should immediately hit the pot again with a new number. Any youth who are left over after groups have formed must stand on the edge of the playing area until all but two players remain in the game.

SHaRe anD CaRe GR⊙UPS

Checking in: Highs and lows of the week, prayer requests, and prayer

Warm up: Ask participants to think about a time when they felt truly forgiven. How did they respond to God? To others around them?

Have iT Y⊙UR Way!
Choose from, adapt, or rearrange these elements to create the best soul feast for your youth group.

THe FiXiN'S
More fun stuff to make the theme extra special! Your choice.

Munchies

Bring supplies and allow the youth to decorate cupcakes or sugar cookies. If anyone is dissatisfied with the initial outcome, he or she can start over!

Popular Songs

Use these before and/or after the program to engage the youth. These are some options. Try to include the latest appropriate popular songs.

• "Irene," by Toby Mac (*Momentum*)

Worship and Praise Music

• "You Are My King (Amazing Love)," by Newsboys (*Adoration: The Worship Album*)
• "Lord, Have Mercy," by Michael W. Smith (*Worship Again*)
• "Merciful Rain," by FFH (*City on a Hill*)
• "Grace Like Rain," by Todd Agnew (*Grace Like Rain*)

Other Movie Options

Choose one of the movies suggested, or ask students to recommend a more recent release. Be sure to preview your selection to avoid any content that would be objectionable in your setting. Remember that you must have a video license.
(Video licensing information on CD)

• *The Cell* (R) (2000)
• *Bedazzled* (2000)

Leader Scripture Exploration

• **Romans 6:1-14** (Dying to sin; rising to life in Christ)
• **Luke 14:15-23** (The great banquet)

On Screen

Key points of presentation (PowerPoint® on CD)

On-the-Street Interviews

Have the youth videotape random youth at the mall (or random church members at various church functions); ask this question: What do you have to do to earn God's forgiveness? (End the tape with your pastor or someone the youth know and trust stating that we can never "earn" God's forgiveness. God offers it to us without cost—a free gift—because God loves us.)

Out and About

Set up a banquet for your youth and have this meeting at the banquet table. End the program with a celebration that, because we are forgiven, all are invited to the banquet with Christ. All we need to do is accept Jesus' invitation to that banquet.

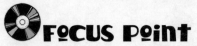

Focus Point

Video Option: *City Slickers* (1991). Billy Crystal's character reminds his friend Phil of when they were children and they were playing ball. If the ball got stuck in a tree, they would call, "Do over." Billy Crystal tells Phil that his life is a clean slate, a "do-over" (Start 1:23:40; stop 1:24:20).

Drama Option: In advance, ask team of students to read the Scripture and create a brief drama that would illustrate Jesus' point. Have them use contemporary settings. A really good resource for showing how to do drama based on Scripture is *Worship Feast Dramas*. (Information on CD)

Focus Thoughts (Text on CD)

Do you know the story from the Gospel of Luke about the woman who gave Jesus a bath? It's in **Luke 7:36-50.** Jesus was a dinner guest at a Pharisee's house when a woman who was known as a sinner came to see Jesus. She brought with her a jar of ointment, and when she saw Jesus, the woman began weeping at his feet. Luke says that she began bathing Jesus' feet with her tears and wiping her tears away with her hair. Then she began kissing Jesus' feet and anointing them with the ointment she had brought.

The Pharisee, whose name was Simon, wondered why Jesus would allow this sinner to do such a thing or to even be in Jesus' presence. That's when Jesus spoke up and told a short story, or parable.

Jesus' parable was about a man who had loaned two men some money. One of the men had borrowed five hundred silver pieces—about a year and a half's wages. The other man had borrowed fifty silver pieces—not quite two months' wages. The lender discovered that both men could not pay back the loan; so out of the graciousness of his heart, the man who loaned the money cancelled both the debts. The men owed him nothing.

Jesus asked Simon, "Which of these men loved the lender more?"

How would you have answered? Simon thought a while and said that he'd guess that the one who loved the lender the most would be the one who had the larger debt that was cancelled—the one who had owed the five hundred silver pieces. Jesus agreed.

Then Jesus turned to the woman who was still there crying at his feet and began comparing her to Simon the Pharisee. Jesus reminded Simon that since he had come into the house, Simon had given no water for Jesus to wash his feet; yet the woman had been washing his feet with her tears since she had arrived. Simon had given Jesus no kiss of greeting, but the woman had still not stopped kissing Jesus' feet. Simon did not anoint Jesus' head with oil, but the woman—the sinner—had anointed Jesus' feet with ointment.

The woman's sins, which were many, had been forgiven. Because of that, she showed great love. She gave more thanks, because more was forgiven.

When we become aware of our sins—the terrible things we've done as well as the little things that really are not so trivial if they go against God's will—we can do one of two things: 1) We can deny that we really did anything wrong by making excuses or casting blame on someone else. Or 2) we can confess that God knows best, that we made a mistake, and that we will keep on making mistakes unless we allow Christ to act through us.

Confession is an important part of healing. When the body is sick, it heals more quickly when we recognize the illness and seek to get rid of it. It's the same with our spirits. When we are sinners, we've got to quit ignoring the sin and confess that sin before God. God has promised that we are forgiven. We just need to accept that forgiveness.

Psalm 32:3, 5 is a great Scripture that shows the goodness of confession and God's forgiveness. (*Read aloud the Scripture.*)

If you have made mistakes around sexual relationships with someone else, or if you do in the future, I hope you'll always remember that God makes things new by forgiveness. There is nothing you can do that is stronger than God's love. Listen to this Scripture. (*Read aloud **Romans 8:35, 37-39.***)

That means that God's love is more powerful than any sin you can commit. Stop feeling guilty. Stop allowing that guilt to bring you down. Recognize your sin, confess it to God, and let God take it away so that you can begin to live a life of newness and love. That's the abundant life that Jesus came to give you. Let's pray.

FOCUS GROUP
- What might be the result of refusing to accept God's forgiveness for a particular sin or mistake? What happens when a person is able to confess and let God forgive it?
- Which is easier—to forgive someone else or to forgive yourself? Why?
- Who controls your feelings when you refuse to forgive another person?
- What would help you forgive yourself? What would help you forgive others?
- How does knowing that when you mess up, you can be forgiven affect how you live? Do you feel like you can just go ahead and do whatever you want? Why, or why not?

CLOSING

Psalm 32 Litany (Handout on CD)

Make a Commitment (Service on CD)

Consider repeating the commitment service from the previous meeting (page 50). Invite all of those who made a commitment to abstinence then to hold up their hands with the ring or wristband reminder. You may wish to ask (in advance) at least one guy and one girl to tell why they made the commitment. Then invite the other students to wear the ring or wristband. Remind all that God gives new beginnings when we confess our sin and seek forgiveness. Explain that this is a new commitment that makes no requirements of how well they have held to that commitment in the past. Taking on the ring (or the wristband) is a symbol not of the past, but of the future. End in a prayer, asking God for strength to avoid sexual temptation.

Youth Witness Statement
Ask a youth or two (or college-age person) in your church to talk candidly with the students about a time when he or she experienced God's grace and forgiveness.

Special
Close with a love feast around a table, sharing bread and juice and reminding each other that God's love for us means that we are forgiven and saved while we were sinners. We do not have to become perfect in order for God to love us or forgive us. God's perfect love can fulfill our deepest desire for intimacy. (If a pastor is available, consider celebrating Holy Communion around the table in place of the love feast.)

ROaD TRiP!

At THE CROSSROaDS

A car, a driver, a friend—what do you have? A road trip! Getting a driver's license is a rite of passage and point of great excitement for most youth. Young drivers often feel increased independence and also realize the responsibility of driving a several ton machine. Similarly, as youth encounter bigger issues and decisions in their lives, they need to decide which road to follow.

 ## APPETiZERS

Publicity Ideas: *Invite more youth to the Christian journey. Select any or all of the ideas below. Combine or simplify.*

☺ Using posterboard or heavy cardboard (an appliance box, perhaps), create a signboard in the shape of a car or truck. Ask for two volunteers from the active youth who are willing to wear the signboard to church to get people's attention about the new theme.

☺ Cut out photos of cars from magazines; glue them to construction paper; then write the meeting dates, time, and place, plus a contact phone number on the paper. Hand out two or three of these to group members so they can give them to friends who do not regularly attend your group.

☺ Advertise in your church bulletin, youth newsletter, and on posters around church, using statements such as: "Do you like to travel to exotic places? Join us for a ROAD TRIP!" "We're going places!" or "Driving lessons available!"

☺ Ask for youth volunteers to make an announcement in church and at Sunday school.

☺ Use old maps or download and make copies of a map to your meeting place. Send to all of the youth in the church the map, with "Road Trip!" written across it. Add the date, time, place, and "See you there!"

💿 Print out the poster (<u>Design on CD</u>) the size of a postcard. Glue it onto a large index card, write the meeting information on it, and mail it to members and prospective members. Print several and use them for other events as well, since the emphasis of "We'll fit you in!" applies to more than just the Road Trip theme.

COMBOS MENU

Main Dishes

Weekly Program Options: *Choose one or all; do in any order. Check each description for variations and the fixin's. Invite a team of youth to decide how to personalize each program.*

1. **Driving Lessons**—Before someone learns to drive, he or she needs to know some basic rules of the road and how to handle a car. In the Christian life, there are also some "basics" to know and understand.

2. **Destination**—Heaven is our final destination, but where do we want to go on the way there? How do we act, make decisions, live the life we have here on earth?

3. **Following the Signs**—What are some of the signs we follow as Christians? How do we know which way to go?

4. **Sharing the Road**—Just as drivers must get along with other motorists, Christians live in community with other believers. What does it mean to share the road and the journey of faith?

Spice It Up

Theme Decorations: *Look at your space. Use your imagination. Enlist several youth to help decorate the meeting room.*

- Make a worship center with a road map, small toy cars, a stretch of track or road from a block set, a copy of your state's driving test, a Bible, and a large cross.

- Pull out your red, yellow, and black paint cans. Make some large road signs: Stop, yield, one way, go, U-turn, road narrows, no outlet, end, use low gear, bump, do not enter, curvy road. share the road, road construction ahead, no stopping any time, slippery road, dip, road closed, detour. Give them away as prizes. (Sign design source on CD)

- Create special signs that lead to your meeting space; use them in newsletters and bulletins as well:

  • DO NOT PASS up this opportunity to grow closer to God
  • YIELD to the Greater Power
  • STOP and get to know God

- Have the theme logo made into a big banner, and hang it on the wall. (Theme logo on CD)

DRINKS

" 'Lord, when was it that we saw you . . . thirsty and gave you something to drink? . . .' 'Truly, I tell you, just as you did it to one of the least of these' " (Matthew 25:37, 40a).

Service project ideas

DRIVING LESSONS

Have It Your Way!

Choose from, adapt, or rearrange these elements to create the best soul feast for your youth group.

The Fixin's

More fun stuff to make the theme extra special! Your choice.

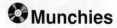

Munchies

- Find a car or truck-shaped cookie cutter and make sugar cookies for the group. Icing in the details is optional.
  (Additional ideas on CD)

Popular Songs

Use these before and/or after the program to engage the youth. These are some options. Try to include the latest appropriate popular songs.

- "Drive My Car," by the Beatles (*Drive My Car*)
- "Drive My Car," by David Crosby (*Oh Yes I Can*)

Worship and Praise Music

- "O Praise Him (All This for a King)" by Passion (*Sacred Revolution: Songs From One Day '03*)
- "Shout to the North," by Delirious (*Worship Together: I Could Sing of Your Love Forever*)
- "I Want to Know You (In the Secret)" by SonicFlood (*I Could Sing of Your Love Forever 2*)
- "Every Move I Make," by David Crowder Band (*The Lime CD*)

SOUL FOOD: Love is what drives Christians.

SCRIPTURE: Matthew 5:43-48 (Love your enemies.); Matthew 22:34-40 (Love God and neighbor.); John 13:34-35 (Love one another.)

Games (Additional game on CD)

If I Were a Car . . .

Hand out paper to the group members (sitting in a circle) and ask them to put their name in large letters at the top of the sheet. Then say, "If I were a car, what model would I be? And what kind of car would you be? We're going to find out what other people might guess for us." As you give the following instructions, remind the youth that this game is to be in the spirit of good fun:

- Each person writes at the bottom of his or her paper the kind of car he or she imagines that he or she would be and then folds up the bottom of the paper to hide the answer.

- Then pass the paper to the person on the right. The next person sees whose paper it is, writes what kind of car that person might be, folds the bottom up to cover the answer, then passes the paper on to the person on the right.

- This sequence continues until each person receives his or her paper back. Then each person unfolds his or her paper and reads the other guesses.

- Give two prizes: to the person with the greatest number of same answers as to which car represents that person, and one for the person whose personal response matches the most other answers.

Car Races

The previous week, enlist the help of members of the group who might still have some small cars (MatchBox, Hot Wheels, and so forth). Ask volunteers to set up a track or an obstacle course for a race that in some way engages all of the group members. This may mean different "heats" of a race on a wooden track, or measuring whose car goes the farthest on a straight stretch, or cars doing aerial tricks. Let some of the youth run with this idea; it may be the first time in years they've been encouraged to play with little cars.

SHARE AND CARE GROUPS

Checking in: Highs and lows of the week, prayer requests, and prayer

Warm up: Get a copy of your state's driver's license exam, and ask the group questions from the book. Divide into teams, making sure that each team has an equal number of students who already have their license, and those who haven't yet taken the test.

FOCUS POINT

Video Options: *The Long, Long Trailer* (1954) (Start 14:50; stop 17:15). Desi Arnez learns how to drive with a trailer hitched to his car.

Skit Option: Ask for volunteers to act out these skits:

• a teenager on his or her first driving lesson (need driver, teacher, and another student in the back seat)
• a driver with only a learner's permit drives on the freeway for the first time, with his or her mom or dad in the passenger seat
• a new driver is pulled over by a cop for speeding
• a student driver tries to parallel park for the first time

FOCUS THOUGHTS (Text on CD)

Anytime we learn something new, we must follow basic rules. When a person learns to drive, for instance, it's crucial to remember to keep your eyes on the road, hold the steering wheel with a steady hand, put your foot on the brake to stop, stop in time to avoid hitting something.

What are some other important rules to know if you are going to drive a car? (*Ask the youth for their ideas.*)

This week we're using "driving lessons" as an analogy for the "basics" we need to know about the Christian life. Jesus has given us five basic "rules" for living the abundant life he promised:

1. **Love God.** This is our starting point. It makes sense because we know that God loved us first. God wants us to take advantage of, revel in, thoroughly enjoy being loved. The way we do that is simply to love God in return. The more wholeheartedly we love God (with heart, soul, strength, and mind), the more we will find ourselves blessed. To love God is the first commandment; it came even before Jesus. We find it first in the Old Testament.

2. **Love your neighbor.** In response to a question, Jesus said that loving God was the first great commandment, and the second was to love our neighbor. Then he told a story to help us understand who our neighbor is. Do you remember that one? (*Good Samaritan*) Now, just as then, Jesus often surprises us with reminders of who "our neighbors" are. In God's eyes, anyone in need is our neighbor.

3. **Love yourself.** Many times people overlook this important part of the Greatest Commandments. Let's listen carefully to the whole Scripture. (*Read aloud Matthew 22:36-39, emphasizing "as yourself."*)

Driving Lessons

Other Movie Options

Choose one of these movies, or ask students to recommend a more recent release. Be sure to preview your selection to avoid any content that would be objectionable in your setting. Remember you must have a video license.
(Video licensing information on CD)

• *Herbie Rides Again* (1974)
• *Driving Miss Daisy* (1990)

Create a Video

Ask family (or other older friends) to tell the story of how they learned to drive. Or simply have several youth interview without videoing and then retell some of the funniest moments they heard of driving lessons.

Talk Tip

Invite a student or two to act out the list of things "crucial to remember" as you say them. Have your actors practice briefly in advance and be ready to "ham it up."

• Keep your eyes on the road.
• Hold the steering wheel with a steady hand.
• Put your foot on the brake to stop.
• Stop in time to avoid hitting something.

Leader Scripture Exploration

• **Deuteronomy 6:1-9** (The Shema: Love God)
• **Luke 10:25-37** (The Good Samaritan)

On Screen

Key points in Focus Thoughts
(PowerPoint® on CD)

Out and About

If your community has an amusement park, take the group to go for a ride on the kiddie or bumper cars. Or take an instant or digital camera to a shopping center that has a car ride for little kids. Snap some photos of each group member hamming it up while "driving" the car.

Service Projects

Have the group spend an hour at a preschool or kindergarten class, reading stories one-on-one with children. Encourage all of the youth readers to find car and truck books (always favorites with young children) to let the younger kids point out their favorite vehicles. Have them put together puzzles of vehicles or play cars and trucks with the children. Talk afterward about how the activity fits with Jesus' love commandments.

Youth Witness Statement

Invite a student to talk about his or her experience with living by the love rules. He or she could focus on any one or two of the commandments. (How-to on CD)

Poster

We'll fit you in! (Design on CD)

Art Project

Have the youth make a *mezuzah*. Many Jewish families have Deuteronomy 6:4-5 (the *Shema*), written out on a slip of parchment inside a metal or wooden box called a *mezuzah*, which is attached to a doorway of their home. Jews often touch the mezuzah as they enter or leave their house. Supply the youth with small boxes (jewelry size) or tins, plus paints or markers and so on for decorating with. Invite the youth to post their mezuzah on a doorway in their home as a reminder.

Why would Jesus slip that statement in there? Think about the message of the Bible: God loves us. God counts us as God's own children. We are valued. It makes sense then that we should value ourselves. That doesn't mean having a puffed up, conceited view of who we are—but a real sense that we are special because God the Creator of all, God the Almighty, loves us. God knows everything about us and still loves us. So we too should value who we are and take care of ourselves. In that way, we honor the God who has created us.

4. **Love one another.** Jesus had a group of close friends, among them were the people we call the Disciples. Jesus knew that his time on earth was coming to an end. He began giving instructions to his close followers. (*Read aloud **John 13:34-35.***) Notice the last line: "By this everyone will know that you are my disciples." One of the biggest reasons Christianity has grown and lasted for more than twenty centuries is the witness of how Christians love one another. Think of the very best image you can of family love. Christians extend that kind of respect and caring to include their brothers and sisters in Christ.

5. **Love your enemies.** Jesus wasn't just a "nice guy." He was actually pretty radical. He had a habit of turning people's preconceived notions upside down and inside out. It's no wonder that people flocked to hear what he had to say. One of the biggest surprises came in his Sermon on the Mount. The whole sermon is filled with some pretty radical stuff, but perhaps the most challenging was his commandment to "love your enemies." (*Read aloud **Matthew 5:43-48.***)

In identifying these five "love commandments," Jesus gives us a glimpse of God, who loves perfectly. Jesus is calling us to live by these basic rules as we drive forward into life. Let's pray.

FOCUS GROUP

• How can we live out each of the love commandments? Make a list of at least five specific examples for each commandment or choose one or two commandments and make a longer list. If you have time, make a second list of specific things that Christians would not do if they were following the particular love commandment.
• On a practical day-to-day basis, what is the most challenging aspect of following Jesus' commandments?

CLOSING

Hand out index cards and give time for the youth to write their own version of the "basics" (Jesus' love commandments). Encourage the youth to put this card someplace that will remind them of their call as Christians. Tell the group that devout Jewish people pray the *Shema,* the first commandment, (**Deuteronomy 6:4-5**) when they wake in the morning and before they go to sleep at night. They also post it on the doorways of their homes and touch it as a reminder when they pass through the door. Invite the youth to commit to saying their summary version of Jesus' commandments in the morning and at night or when they leave or enter their bedroom or home.

Close with prayer that emphasizes that we love because God first loved us.

Destination

SOUL FOOD: Our destination as Christians makes a difference in the journey.

SCRIPTURE: Philippians 3:12-14 (I press on toward the goal.)

**Games** (Additional game on CD)

Destination Tag

When whoever is "It" tags another person in this traditional game, the tagged one has to yell out the name of a destination (place one could travel to) before It counts to five. If the one tagged doesn't yell out a destination in time, he or she becomes It.

Journey Together

Sit in a circle and together tell the story of a journey your group might take together. Each person contributes a sentence to your group's (made up) story, adding a detail to whatever the previous person has suggested.

SHARE AND CARE GROUPS

Checking in: Highs and lows of the week, prayer requests, and prayer

Warm up: Ask various youth to name three places they hope to visit one day. Ask: "Why do these destinations appeal to you? If you decided to go on a trip, what would you do in order to find your destination? In general, is the journey (the "getting there") or the destination (arrival) more important for you?"

FOCUS POINT

Video Option: *Tuesdays With Morrie* (1999). Use one or both of these scenes: 47:34–48:32 (cut when a hand appears on screen) and 52:40–55:50 (end when the tape recorder is turned off). This movie in its entirety complements the theme and would provoke good discussion.

Or read the scenes as written in the book, *Tuesdays With Morrie: An Old Man, a Young Man, and Life's Greatest Lesson,* by Mitch Albom (Hardback: Doubleday, 1997; ISBN: 0385484518; Paperback: Broadway Books; ISBN: 076790592X) (in one edition: the last paragraph on page 80–the second paragraph on page 85 and the second paragraph on page 126–the sixth paragraph on page 128. Or ask group members to read the book ahead of time for discussion.)

Have It Your Way!

Choose from, adapt, or rearrange these elements to create the best soul feast for your youth group.

THE FIXIN'S

More fun stuff to make the theme extra special! Your choice.

**Munchies**

Decorate with the flags of different "destination" countries or display a world map with pushpins marking chosen countries. This snack could be a fun way for youth to try new foods. You might have families of the youth who could share their culture's favorite recipes. Enlist some of the youth to choose and prepare or buy foods. You may be surprised at some of their favorites.
(Examples on CD)

Popular Songs

Use these before and/or after the program to engage the youth. These are some options. Try to include the latest appropriate popular songs.

- "Traveling Again (Traveling 1)" by Dar Williams (*The Honesty Room*)
- "Road to Nowhere," by the Talking Heads (*The Best of the Talking Heads*)
- "Further On (Up the Road)" by Bruce Springsteen (*The Rising*)
- "Destination Anywhere," by Jon Bon Jovi (*Destination Anywhere*)
- "In the Journey," by Martin Sexton (*In the Journey*)

Worship and Praise Music

- "I'm Waiting for You," by Michael W. Smith (*I'll Lead You Home*)
- "I Want Jesus to Walk With Me," by the Holmes Brothers (*Jubilation*)
- "Live Right," by Rich Mullins (*Rich Mullins*)

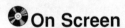Other Movie Options

Choose one of these, or ask students to recommend a more recent release. Be sure to preview your selection to avoid any content that would be objectionable in your setting. Remember that you must have a video license.
(Video licensing information on CD)

Middle School
- *The Road to Bali* (1953)
- *Road to Morocco* (1942)

High School
- *Smoke Signals* (1998)
- *The Reivers* (1969)
- *National Lampoon's Vacation* (R) (1983)

Leader Scripture Exploration

- **Acts 7:54–8:3** (Saul persecutes the church.)
- **Acts 9:1-19** (Saul meets Christ.)
- **Philippians 3:2-16** (Christ is the ultimate goal.)

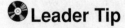On Screen

Key points in Focus Thoughts (PowerPoint® on CD)

Leader Tip

Print the Focus Group questions from the CD and give copies to key youth. Have them lead the discussion in the focus groups. These youth will develop their leadership skills as well as encourage thoughtful reflection.
(Focus Group questions on CD)

Skit Option: Ask for three volunteers to improvise a skit about three people going on a trip together. Then ask for others in the group to suggest 1) a destination, 2) means of transportation, 3) reason for the trip. You might have some simple props available. This skit could be repeated with other volunteers and suggestions.

FOCUS THOUGHTS (Text on CD)

Do you know where you're going? How many of you have been thinking about what you will do after high school? (*Ask for a show of hands.*) At this point in your lives, you may not know: Will it be college? a job? technical school? volunteer work with Americorps? going into the military?

(*Invite volunteers to say in a few words or short sentence what they consider their destination. Accept each answer nonjudgmentally.*)

"What will I do when I grow up? Where will I go? What will I be?" These are important questions. They're questions of what's my destination, what's my goal? Our society puts so much emphasis on destinations such as graduating from high school, getting accepted at a good college, getting a good job, being a financial success that it's easy to forget that life is also about the journey, as well as the destination. Life is about both where we're going and how we choose to get there.

For those of us who follow Jesus, that's especially true. Think of it this way: Jesus came to live on earth so that we might know God in a new way. He knew that after his earthly journey was through, he would return to live with God in eternity. In other words, eternal life was his ultimate destination.

But on the way, in his earthly days, Jesus knew that he would face misunderstanding, persecution, and even death on the cross. Along the way, he kept his eyes on the ultimate destination and lived fully in the journey. Jesus spent his earthly days teaching, praying, preaching, healing, being present with people, and truly living in the moments given to him. Knowing his destination, he could say no to distractions and wrong turns and an enthusiastic YES to the journey that would take him home—even when the way was hard.

Knowing where you want to go makes the difference. Jesus invites you to choose life—eternal life with him as the destination and abundant life with him on the journey. Let's pray.

FOCUS GROUP (Text on CD)

- If you choose life in Christ (in eternity and now), how does that destination help you with your day-to-day journey? How does it influence your choices? Give some examples?
- How would your day-to-day life be different if you didn't care about being with Christ (in eternity and now)? Refer to the examples from the previous question; add some others.

*(Read aloud **Philippians 3:12-14**.)*

- Paul used the example of his own life in this letter to the church at Philippi. He talked about "forgetting what was in the past." What do you know about Paul's life before meeting Christ that he would have had regrets about? What kinds of "past" might stop persons from feeling that they could choose life with Christ as a destination (in eternity and now)? What do you think Christ would say to those concerns?

- Jesus' life on earth was not easy. He was misunderstood by his friends, persecuted for his beliefs and teachings, tortured and killed. Being a Christ-follower does not guarantee an easy life. How do you think having life with Christ as the goal will help us "press on" even in the midst of suffering?

CLOSING

Where Am I Now?

For this activity, you will need: old maps, cut into sections at least 10-by-10. The maps may be from any state or country; but each section needs to have a large selection of place names (cities, rivers, mountains), and it's good if there are a variety of places represented. If you don't have old maps on hand, you could go online to find maps to print out.

Give all of the group members a section of map. Invite them to look over the map for place names that describe (symbolically) where they are now and where they are going. For instance, a youth with a section of the South Dakota map might think that she is in Deadwood (not much going on in her life), Rapid City (too much happening), Driftwood (just drifting along with no ambition), or Porcupine (not letting people get close). She might choose Big Bend (ready for change), Loyalton (strive to be loyal to Jesus), Garden City (heaven), or Goodwin (the good in me will win out).

When everyone has chosen his or her two place names, give everyone a chance to tell about what he or she chose and why.

Blessing for the Journey

Darken the room. Then light a candle to place in the middle of your meeting space. Remind the youth that wherever they are, they are not alone; the light of Christ shines in the darkness as a beacon, as a goal, as a destination. Paul reminds us that we can forget our past, thanks to God's gracious love for us. We can press on toward the light and live in the Christ light forever.

On-the-Street Interview

Take a poll of people on the street or ask congregants after a worship service, "Where in the world do you want to travel? Why?" Bring a world map to your group meeting and use pushpins to chart the destinations.

Out and About

What are the best known destinations in your community? Make a list of places your town is known for, then visit each place to take a group photo. Arrange the photos in a collage to display in your meeting room.

Service Projects

Think of several projects as "destinations." Vote on which project the group chooses to serve. If there's a tie, split into two groups (if you have enough adults and transportation), Then come back to compare each group's experience in their chosen service.

FOLLOWING THE SIGNS

Have It Your Way!

Choose from, adapt, or rearrange these elements to create the best soul feast for your youth group.

The Fixin's

More fun stuff to make the theme extra special! Your choice.

Munchies

Display appropriately-colored foods next to the three colors of a stop light. (You might make a cardboard stop light for the food table.)

- Red foods could include red bell pepper strips, red licorice, red apple slices, cherries, tomatoes, watermelon, red grapes.

- Yellow foods could include lemon meringue pie, bananas, saffron rice, lemonade, lemon cake, cornbread and honey butter, yellow candies.

- Green foods could include celery sticks, green bell pepper strips, broccoli stalks with green-colored dip, pesto pasta, sprouts, macaroni and cheese with green food coloring, green candies.

Popular Songs

Use these before and/or after the program to engage the youth. These are some options. Try to include the latest appropriate popular songs.

- "Signs," by Michael W. Smith (*The Second Decade 1993–2003*)
- "Sky Fits Heaven," by Madonna (*Ray of Light*)
- "Signs," by Creed (*Weathered*)

SOUL FOOD: When we are open to God's leading, the signs are there.

SCRIPTURE: John 20:30-31 (The purpose of the signs)

 GAMES (Additional game on CD)

Mother, May I?

Choose one person to play "Mother." Everyone else lines up in a straight line across the room from Mother. One at a time, others ask permission to take steps toward where Mother stands. For example, someone asks, "Mother, may I take ten baby steps forward?" (Variations are regular steps, giant steps, hopping steps, or any other creative movement.)

Mother answers, "Yes, you may" or "No, you may not," and that person must follow Mother's commands. If a player moves without permission, the player must go back to the starting line. The first person to touch Mother becomes Mother in the next game. Variation: Mother may yell out, "Go!" "Stop!" "Reverse!" or other driving terms.

Treasure Hunt

Design a treasure hunt complete with maps, clues, and a "treasure chest" full of goodies (gold-foil chocolate coins, for example). Divide the youth into teams, set a time limit, hand out the clues, and watch them go.

The treasure hunt is an excellent opportunity to involve parents who may not be able to give consistent time to the youth group but who could design this game. Put them in charge of creating the clues, maps, and treasure chest.

SHARE AND CARE GROUPS

Checking in: Highs and lows of the week, prayer requests, and prayer

Warm up: Ask: What's the oddest road sign you've seen? Does anyone have a funny story about not following directions and getting lost?

 FOCUS POINT

Video Option: *Harry Potter and the Sorcerer's Stone* (2001). Use DVD scene 9: Harry must follow Hagrid's instructions and his ticket to Platform 9¾, ending where Harry sees the train. Harry must interpret unfamiliar signs and trust others in order to go where he needs to go.

Activity Option: Mapping My Life Journey

(Road signs source on CD)

Give each student construction paper, the road signs page, a pair of scissors. Have glue available for every two or three persons to share. Invite the youth to draw their personal life journey (from birth to the present), highlighting the most important events so far. Participants may cut out the road signs or create new ones of their own and draw them or glue them to appropriate sections of their life map. For instance, a rough time could be symbolized by "bump," "blasting zone," or "slippery road." Finding a close friend or romantic partner could be "share the road." Play some of the traveling songs (page 59) in the background as youth work on this project.

Allocate a good chunk of time for this activity so that youth can reflect on where they've been as they create the life map. Take time for volunteers to talk about their map with their small group—or the whole group, if desired.

 Focus Thoughts (Text on CD)

Young children learn to recognize the shape and color of a stop sign. Preschool and kindergarten teachers often use traffic lights as a teaching tool to help young children learn basic colors. So when the children grow old enough to learn to drive, they have a head start in knowing the different signs that will help them navigate the road safely.

What road signs do we know by heart? *(Invite student responses.)*

Sometimes the signs we need to read are not so obvious as a stop sign or the top color of a traffic light. Throughout history God has used many ways to communicate with humanity. Let's look at a familiar story to see how God communicated with two groups of very different people.

*(Retell the story of the shepherds, **Luke 2:8-20**. Point out that they were poor, unclean, and on the fringe of society. Most people did not want to associate with them. Point out also that God chose to announce the birth of the Savior of the world, not in a palace—a place of power and wealth, but in a field to the poor and marginalized people of society—the shepherds. Draw attention to how the shepherds responded to the good news [going, worshiping, praising].)*

*(Retell the story of the wise men, **Matthew 2:1-12, 16**. Point out that they, in contrast to the shepherds, had wealth and power. But unlike Herod, who also had wealth and power, they were seekers; and when they saw the sign of the star, they responded by going to find the new king [at considerable effort] and to worship him. Herod contrasts with the wise men. When he was told [a pretty direct sign!], he felt threatened, tried to deceive the wise men, and ultimately committed the murder of hundreds of innocent children.)*

These two stories of following the signs have much to tell us:

• **God gives signs to all of us**—rich and poor, powerful and marginalized.

• **We have to be open to seeing the signs.** We can be actively seeking (like the wise men) or willing to believe what we hear and see (like the shepherds).

Worship and Praise Music

• "The First Noel"
• "We Three Kings"
• "Angels We Have Heard on High"
• "I Can Only Imagine," by MercyMe (*Almost There*)

Other Movie Options

Choose *Harry Potter and the Sorcerer's Stone* (2001), or ask students to recommend a more recent release. Be sure to preview your selection to avoid any content that would be objectionable in your setting. Remember that you must have a video license. (Video licensing information on CD)

Leader Scripture Exploration

• **Matthew 1:18-25** (Joseph's decision)
• **Matthew 2:1-12** (The wise men)
• **Matthew 2:16-18** (Herod's response)
• **Luke 1:46-55** (Mary's Magnificat)
• **Luke 2:8-20** (The shepherds)

On Screen

Key points in Focus Thoughts (PowerPoint® on CD)

Talk Tip

Retelling the stories of the shepherds and of the wise men is a good opportunity for student involvement. Consider dividing the group in half, giving each group one of the stories to read. Then have the students help you retell the two stories. You may invite students to present the story in some fashion (verbal report, skit, readers theater), have them "fill in the blanks" that you create in telling the story, or use a question-and-answer format. Or combine styles.

Out and About

Create a walking tour of your area in which teams of youth must carefully follow directions. For example, "Turn left at the church entrance sign, go to the second Yield sign, and turn right." Have munchies ready at the destination (perhaps the home of a youth group member or the pastor), or end up at an ice cream parlor to enjoy something cold before returning to the church.

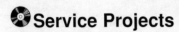 Service Projects

If Christmas time is near, consider developing a live nativity scene for your congregation and community. (Additional idea on CD)

Worship Token

Give each youth a Christmas card as a reminder of this message. Sign the card and write a personal message if you choose.

- **Signs call for action.** The shepherds responded to the invitation to see the Savior; the wise men undertook a long journey in faith that they would find the one they were seeking. They were willing to disrupt their routines in order to participate in God's marvelous action.

- **God gives us a choice.** We can be like Herod, who not only turned away from the opportunity, but chose to do evil. Or we can be like the wise men, the shepherds, and even the angels and praise and worship!

In the Gospel of John, we find many more stories of Jesus as a grown man. He chose to live in ways that reveal God to humanity. His teachings, his healings, his miracles, his death, his resurrection are all signs beckoning us to follow.

(*Read aloud* **John 20:30-31.**)

"These are written that you may come to believe . . . and that through believing you may have life in his name." Jesus is God's greatest sign to us. Believe and have life blessed by him. Let's pray.

 FOCUS GROUP (Alternative option on CD)

- Although God may not send a host of angels, a star, or a dream to us, what are some of the signs we follow as Christians? What are some of the ways God "talks" to people? (*Scripture, the counsel of other Christians, our inner feelings or instincts, prayer*)
- How can we be open to ways God might choose to communicate with us?
- How might we prepare ourselves to respond to whatever God asks of us?
- How can we support one another as we each seek to listen to God and pay attention to whatever signs come?

CLOSING

At the Stable

Have a nativity set at the worship center. Invite the youth to gather around. As you talk, pick up the various pieces of the set. Briefly tell about Mary, the teenage girl who responded with praise and courage; Joseph, who gave loving support; the angels, who burst forth with joy; the shepherds, who traded fear for praise; the wise men, who found what they were seeking; Jesus, who is our greatest sign guiding us to a blessed life.

Invite the students to picture themselves at the stable. Close with a time of prayer at the altar or kneeling before the worship center with the nativity scene. You may wish to play "I Can Only Imagine," by MercyMe, or a medley of Christmas carols during the prayer time.

Benediction

Read aloud **Proverbs 3:5-6** as a reminder of how in trusting God we find guidance for our journey.

SHARING THE ROAD

SOUL FOOD: The Christ road leads to harmony; we are witnesses inviting others to travel this road.

SCRIPTURE: Colossians 3:12-15 (Bear with one another.)

GAMES (Additional games on CD)

Machine

Divide the youth into groups of four or five. Ask each group to invent and act out a machine where each person has a movement and a sound that integrates into the whole machine. You don't need to be any more specific than that. Leave this open-ended so that youth can be creative and funny.

Architects

Let the youth arrange themselves into groups of three or four. Give each group a set of building materials such as Jenga® blocks, a can of play dough, pile of twigs, building blocks—whatever you have on hand that could be used to build. All of the groups should have identical sets of supplies.

They should work together to create a tower from the supplies and give their tower a name that represents the way the group worked together to create it.

SHARE AND CARE GROUPS

Checking in: Highs and lows of the week, prayer requests, and prayer

Warm up: Tell of a positive team experience you've had. What kinds of learnings does one get in participating on a team (sports, mission, or other kind of team)? If you could invent a new team sport, what skills would it require? How many players?

Video Option: *Whale Rider* (2003). Show DVD Scene 26: The community surrounds the young girl as they celebrate their culture and history.

Have It YOUR WaY!

Choose from, adapt, or rearrange these elements to create the best soul feast for your youth group.

THE FIXIN'S

More fun stuff to make the theme extra special! Your choice.

Munchies

Choose foods that are meant for sharing, such as:

• Twin-Popsicles®
• Apple slices and peanut butter
• Tortilla chips and salsa
• Popcorn
• Raw veggies and ranch dressing
• Cookies and milk

(The week before, you might ask your group to come up with their own list of foods that are meant to be shared. Ask the youth to volunteer to bring in their suggested foods.)

Popular Songs

Use these before and/or after the program to engage the youth. These are some options. Try to include the latest appropriate popular songs.

• "On the Road Again," by Willie Nelson (*16 Biggest Hits*)
• "Where Your Road Leads," by Trisha Yearwood, with Garth Brooks (*Where Your Road Leads*)
• "Road Trippin'," by the Red Hot Chili Peppers (*Greatest Hits*)
• "October Road," by James Taylor (*October Road*)
• "Let's Take a Ride," by Justin Timberlake (*Justified*)
• "Road Rash," by the Mad Caddies (*Duck and Cover*)

Worship and Praise Music

- "Lean on Me"
- "They'll Know We Are Christians by Our Love"
- "Jesu, Jesu, Fill Us With Your Love"
- "We Are a Rainbow"

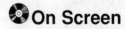Other Movie Options

Choose one of these, or ask students to recommend a more recent release. Be sure to preview your selection to avoid any content that would be objectionable in your setting. Remember that you must have a video license.
(Video licensing information on CD)

Middle School
- *The Adventures of Milo and Otis* (1989)
- *Harry Potter and the Sorcerer's Stone* (2001)
- *Homeward Bound: The Incredible Journey* (1993)

High School
- *Bill and Ted's Excellent Adventure* (1989)
- *Butch Cassidy and the Sundance Kid* (1969)
- *Forces of Nature* (1999)
- *The Lord of the Rings: The Return of the King* (2003)

Leader Scripture Exploration

- **Galatians 6:2-10** (Bear one another's burdens.)
- **Ephesians 4:1-5** (Bear with one another in love.)

On Screen

Key points in Focus Thoughts
(PowerPoint® on CD)

Role Play Option: Choose a few of these role plays to get started; then consider coming back to the list again as part of the Focus Group. (List on CD)

- One youth group member ignores another, less popular member at school.
- A group member divulges information that was supposed to be kept confidential in the group.
- Two group members who are a couple break up, and other group members are tempted to take sides.
- On a group work project, it is clear that not everyone is pulling their weight in getting the job done.
- Someone suddenly stops coming to group meetings.
- Two best friends make the rest of the group feel left out.
- Some group members are rude to an adult group leader.
- One person sees another group member engaging in negative behaviors at a party.

FOCUS THOUGHTS (Text on CD)

How many of you know what "road rage" is? (*Ask for a show of hands.*) You're driving along and suddenly something unexpected happens, which is often the case when driving. You react quickly; and in doing so, cut another driver off without meaning to. Now you have a new problem: The other guy is angry. Road rage!

Driving is a lot like life. Things are going along more or less OK; and then WHAM, something happens that no one expected. You react. The other person reacts, and things "blow up." Road rage is just one example, but the news is full of violence at many levels. You may be fortunate enough not to experience violence; but I'm sure that you know anger, hurt, and disappointment first hand.

So what's the solution? Only one person on the highway at a time? Not likely. Human beings are genetically wired to be in community, to relate to other people, to engage in give and take. We all need one another. So we also need to learn how to share this road we call life.

Jesus knew this. He lived and taught ways to live together and love one another. Paul, one of Jesus' followers, wrote numerous letters to the early Christians about this very issue. In his letters, which are now books in our Bible, he emphasized the need to love other people and to put that love into concrete words and deeds. He gave practical advice for people who, although they lived centuries before our time, were like us: They sometimes quarreled, misunderstood one another, said the wrong thing, hurt others, or had their feelings hurt. Let's hear from Paul.

(*Read aloud Colossians 3:12-15.*)

People have choices. Let's go back to our road-rage scene and look at it from the other point of view. If you are the person who nearly got "creamed," you might react with anger and seek vengeance—pay back! Or as a follower of Christ, you can "bear with one another," be humble enough to know you too have made mistakes, forgive the other person, be grateful that things weren't worse, and move on with a sense of peace. You have a choice.

One thing that sets Christians apart is how we practice our faith. We are not believers in a vacuum. Our faith guides us as we listen to our parents, talk to our siblings, hang out with friends, drive down the road. When we live our faith "clothed with compassion, kindness, humility, meekness, and patience," bearing with one another and forgiving (as we have been forgiven), we help make "perfect harmony" for ourselves and others.

Here's one other thing to think about: When we live our lives out of love, we are sharing the road in another sense. We are sharing our faith through the witness of our lives. Through our example, we are inviting others to share the road we have found to love in Christ Jesus. Let's pray.

FOCUS GROUP (Additional idea on CD)

Reread **Colossians 3:12-15.** Do the role plays (Focus Point) in light of these verses. You may replay ones done earlier or choose new ones. If you did not use the role plays earlier, give volunteers the option of playing out the negative as well as the positive (Scripture-based) ways. Then discuss the contrasts.

- Which of Paul's encouraging suggestions are hardest for you to live out?
- Which are more challenging for your particular group?
- Are there specific suggestions that might be good for the group to pledge to work on together?

CLOSING

Cross Roads

Invite the youth to a place where there is a large cross.

We've been using the theme of Road Trip the last few weeks. We've taken "driving lessons" and learned the basic rules from Jesus—the love commandments. We've seen Jesus as both our destination and the best sign for getting there. We've looked at the way to sharing the road with others— the Christ way.

Look at the cross. It could also be an image of two roads coming together. When you are driving down a road and there is an intersection, you have to make a choice: Which way will you go?

You stand at the crossroads and before the cross. You have a choice to make. Will you follow the Christ way?

Invite the youth to a time of prayer, kneeling before the cross.

Art Project

Make a group mural, using large sheets of newsprint or butcher paper. In words and pictures, illustrate the suggestions Paul gives in Colossians about how to be a loving community of faith. Invite volunteers to tell about their creation. Affirm them, and close with prayer.

On-the-Street Interviews

Have the youth take a videocamera to the Department of Motor Vehicles or a busy parking lot at a mall or superstore and ask people as they exit, "What is your biggest gripe about other drivers?" and "What do you consider the most important rule for operating a motor vehicle?"

Out and About

Try a Trust Walk where youth pair up with one acting as guide to the other, whose eyes are blindfolded. Give each partner five minutes to guide the other around a park or playground, then have the partners switch roles. Encourage the youth to give clear directions to keep their partner injury free. Then gather as a group to talk about their experiences.

Service Projects

- Hit the road. Take a weekend road trip; stop along the way to do some type of service.

- Adopt a highway. Provide gloves and large trash bags. Have all of the participants wear brightly-colored clothing; long pants; and comfortable, closed-toe shoes. Contact the highway department. They may provide safety vests and even pick up the filled trash bags.

(Additional project on CD)

BEYOND BELIEF

BIG QUESTIONS

These programs deal with issues that often cause division in the Christian community. Present the facts as you know them as best you can. Tell what you believe. Show respect for the beliefs of others. Ask the youth what they have been taught. Be prepared to lead an open and honest discussion.

This theme will allow your group to wrestle with some very tough questions. Don't be afraid to tackle controversial issues. The youth will respect your attempt and your openness. Do your homework on each subject and be prepared to lead each program. Inform your pastor of the subjects you will be covering; keep her or him in the communication loop.

APPETIZERS (Additional ideas on CD)

Publicity Ideas: *Starting this theme is a great time to promote what your group is doing. These topic will attract some youth with big questions. Make sure that you have an open heart and mind. Show respect toward others, and allow the facts and God to do the rest.*

☺ **Special:** Contact the high school cheerleaders and ask them to come up with a dance to "Jumping in the House of God," by Hog (*Jumping in the House of God,* The World Wide Message Tribe and Friends). Have them kickoff the first night of Beyond Belief at your church. Include in your publicity the fact that the cheerleaders will be there.

☺ **Teaser Video:** You can order space videos from NASA or have one of your students put together a PowerPoint® presentation. You might use the video of Neil Armstrong landing on the moon. Show the presentation as a preview and a teaser for "Beyond Belief"

☺ **Friday Night at the Movies:** Have a special showing of the movie *ET* to kick off the theme. *Star Trek* and *Star Wars* are also options. Do this on the Friday (or Saturday) before beginning the theme on Sunday night. Be sure to promote the upcoming themes at the movie night.

Create flyers or "business cards" (Theme logo on CD), with the information about when and where. Challenge the youth to give them out to friends (and soon-to-be-friends) at school or in the neighborhood. Give a t-shirt to every youth who brings a guest. Give one to the guest too.

DRINKS

" 'Lord, when was it that we saw you ... thirsty and gave you something to drink? . .' 'Truly, I tell you, just as yo did it to one of the least of these' " (Matthew 25:37, 40a)

Service project ideas

COMBO MENU

 **Main Dishes**

Weekly Program Options: *Choose one or all; do in any order. Check each description for variations and the fixin's.*

1. **Good vs. Evil**—The question, "Why do bad things happen to good people?" has caused adults and youth to struggle with their faith in a loving God. Use this time to allow your group to explore the good and bad things that happen in life. Who is responsible when bad things happen? Are there really any good people out there?

2. **God AND Science**—Students often get caught in the conflict between science and religion. The Big Bang Theory and the Theory of Evolution seem to at odds with the Bible's account of Creation. Where's the truth?

3. **What's So Special About Jesus?**—In America all religions are the same to the government and to many people. Students have been taught that all religions lead to the same god, and that all people are free to find their own path to their own god. This program will help you point out some of the differences between Jesus and other religious leaders.

4. **Can This Really Make a Difference in My Life?**—Youth often ask, "Is it possible for Christianity to really make a difference in my life? Is it worth all of the trouble? Can God really use someone like me?" Now is the time to let the truth be known. God really can transform lives. God has been doing it for thousands of years. With your help, the youth can tap into the same unbelievable power source with your help.

 Spice It Up (Additional ideas on CD)

Theme Decorations: *Look at your space. Use your imagination. Give away or auction off purchased decorations as prizes at the end of the week or the theme.*

- You can order a plastic star background and a shooting star arch from www.StumpsProm.com. Get some glow-in-the-dark stars from your local novelty store (such as Spencers); add some glow-in-the-dark paint and have a blast.

- Go to your local floral supply store and purchase big plastic foam balls and paint them to look like the planets.

- You can also find inflatable spacemen at most local party stores. Think about having one spaceman for every senior involved and giving them away when the theme is wrapped up.

- Don't forget twinkling Christmas lights.

- Go beyond belief and give away a car. (More on this on the CD)

GOOD VS. EVIL

Have It Your Way!
Choose from, adapt, or rearrange these elements to create the best soul feast for your youth group.

The Fixin's
More fun stuff to make the theme extra special! Your choice.

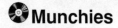 Munchies

- Really Good Chocolate Chip Cookies

Popular Songs

Use these before and/or after the program to engage the youth. These are some options. Try to include the latest appropriate popular songs.

- "Father of Mine," by Everclear (*So Much for the Afterglow*)
- "Not of this World" by Petra (*Not of This World*)
- "Hotel California," by the Eagles (*The Very Best of the Eagles*)
- "Ammunition," by Switchfoot (*The Beautiful Letdown*)
- "Calling All Angels," by Train (*My Private Nation*)

Worship and Praise Music

- "Show Me Your Glory," by Third Day (*Offerings II: All I Have to Give*)
- "Take Me Away," by Delirious (*Touch*)
- "We Exalt Thee," by Petra (*Petra Praise: Rock Cries Out*)
- "God of Wonders," by Third Day (*Offerings II: All I Have to Give*)
- "Sing to the King," by Passion Worship Band (*Sacred Revolution*)
- "Blessed Be Your Name," by Passion Worship Band (*Sacred Revolution*)

SOUL FOOD: In our darkest times, we can trust God to be at work for good and to bring us through the pain—if we love God.

SCRIPTURE: Romans 8:28 (God is at work for good in our lives.); 2 Corinthians 12:9 (God's grace is powerful enough to get us through anything.)

 Games (Additional game on CD)

ET Gotta Eat

Buy some plain M&M®s and some tube socks (one sock for each person playing). Cut two small holes in the socks. Pour a certain number of M&M®s into small bowls (one bowl for each person). Ask for volunteers. Give each person a sock. Have the players place their middle and index fingers through the holes and then eat like ET. Show a video clip from the movie while the game is being played. The first person to eat all of his or her M&M®s wins a huge bag of, what else, M&M®s.

Air Band Contest

Ask your group to come up with an air band performance of their favorite song (appropriate for church). Have a contest. Give bottles of air or cans of air used to clean computers as prizes.

Share and Care Groups

Checking in: Highs and lows of the week, prayer requests, and prayer

Warm up: How do you handle crises? Is it harder to believe in God when things are going bad or going well? Explain your answer. (Additional questions on CD).

Focus Point

Video and Song Option: Have on hand a copy of a 9/11 video and show it to your group (volume off) while playing the song "But If Not" by John Klinepeter (*Alive*). (Video ordering information on CD)

FOCUS THOUGHTS (Text on CD)

I was talking with one of my college buddies recently. He says that he doesn't believe in God, but he always seems to initiate a conversation dealing with religion each time we talk. He recently asked the question that just won't go away, "Why do bad things happen to good people?"

He began by talking about the 30,000 people killed in a recent earthquake. He asked, "How could God allow such a thing?" Then he asked, "How could innocent students be killed at school?" And the barrage continued:

- What about the floods in Asia that killed 100,000 people?
- What about the students killed on a mission trip? How can something that bad happen to so many who are trying to do so much good for God?
- What about AIDS, depression, and suicide?
- What about starvation? How can there be a loving God when all people need is rain? If they had rain in some parts of the world, the people could grow food and millions would not die because they were hungry. Are they being punished? Did they do something wrong?
- How could a loving God allow countless Jews (God's own people) to be tortured and murdered in such an inhumane way during the Holocaust?
- And the whole Hell thing—how could a loving God make someone burn forever?

He said, "Look around—there can't be a God! There is too much pain."

Every day the world falls apart for thousands of people: Devastating medical diagnoses (like cancer), teen pregnancy, divorce, sports injuries, violence, death. It is hard not to ask, "God, why didn't you protect me better? I'm a Christian! Isn't life supposed to be easier?"

I've been able to visit Ground Zero in New York four times. I will never forget watching the television on September 11th— dust, smoke, fire, crumbling buildings, death, people posting pictures of their missing family members and friends. It was so horrible that I could not believe my eyes. On my first visit, all I could think to say was, "No way! God, where were you? How could you let this happen?"

When something goes wrong, we are naturally shocked; we get angry; we look for someone to blame. And God is usually at the top of the short list.

It is important to say, that sometimes human beings are the ones who create bad things. (September 11, for example, was the result of human choice.) I don't believe that God wants tragedy to happen. People choose to do what they will, and as humans we can be very cruel.

Natural disasters, accidents, other things just happen. Again, we look for someone to blame. And when no one else is around, we look at God, point fingers, ask questions, and blast criticisms.

Why do bad things happen to good people? Think about this: "There are no good people. We are all just people." Those are not comforting words, but they may help answer the question. If we are all just people—not good people and bad people—then we are all just people in need of God, who forgives and loves beyond understanding. We all are people in need of God, who judges life not by the moment but by eternity. We are people in need of God, who promises to make good come from bad.

Other Movie Options

Choose one of these other movies, or ask students to recommend a more recent release. Be sure to preview your selection to avoid any content that would be objectionable in your setting. Remember that you must have a video license. (Video licensing information on CD)

- *The Matrix* (R) (1999)
- *The Good Son* (R) (1993)
- *Titanic* (1997)
- *8 Seconds* (1994)
- *The Star Wars Trilogy* (released 2004)
- *Common Threads—Stories From the Quilt* (1989)
- *Wall Street* (R) (1987)

Background Books

Where Is God When It Hurts? and *Bad Stuff in the News* can help you feel prepared for addressing this subject with your group. (Ordering information on CD)

Leader Scripture Exploration

- **Job 38–42:6** (God answers Job.)
- **Matthew 2:16-18** (The male children are ordered to be killed.)
- **Mark 6:1-13** (Jesus is rejected in his own hometown.)
- **Acts 26:1-29** (Paul comes before Agrippa.)
- **Hebrews 3:12-13** (Encourage one another.)

On Screen

Key points in Focus Thoughts (PowerPoint® on CD)

Out and About

- Go to a local comic book store after hours. It's a great place to have a program on good versus evil.

- Do you know anyone going through chemotherapy or dialysis? Ask if you can bring your youth to talk with him or her about the experience. Encourage the patient to speak also about how faith has been helpful. Read the witness statement in this section and you will discover the rewards for your students and the patients.

(Additional idea on CD)

Service Projects

- Turn your group into activists. Research what really goes on in your community. What injustices can you find? Host a rally to communicate your message of love and mercy. Invite other youth groups. Contact your local Christian radio stations and newspapers. Ask your group to come up with a plan to demonstrate the love of Jesus for all peoples. Make sure that you include your pastor, and check with local officials for permission.

- Start an after-school mentoring or tutoring program at a community center or in your church for children who are underprivileged.

Poster (Design on CD)

Make it right through me!

Youth Witness Statement

Have a youth give a 3 to 5 minute testimony on how he or she overcame something bad that happened. (How-to on CD) (Sample witness statement on CD)

Picture this scene: Jesus is praying in the garden, knowing that he was about to be killed; he's actually sweating blood. He even asks God whether there is another way. What happened to him was horrible! And Jesus was more than good!

You and I don't know what the future holds. We can see only a small part of the big picture. But I believe that we can take some strength from the example of Jesus. When things go wrong, pray!

"God I don't understand. This hurts! But, I choose to believe in you. Your will be done. Help me see your picture; help me through this."

The number one phrase in the Bible: "FEAR NOT!" Remember that God promises to be with us when the pieces fall apart, even if we feel totally alone. In **2 Corinthians 12:9,** God promises us "sufficient grace." God's grace is powerful enough to get you through.

In **Romans 8:28,** we have this assurance: "We know that all things work together for good for those who love God, who are called according to God's purposes." When bad things happen in our lives, look back at the bad things that have happened before. Did God help you through those times? Was God faithful? Did you learn anything? How did you grow?

When something bad happens to you, focus on one thing: "I can make it with God's help." Go one step further: Find a way to serve people. Look for broken-hearted people to help. We all have a "Ground Zero" in our lives. When things go wrong, let your prayer be: "Make it right *through* me!"

FOCUS GROUP

- What has happened in your life that has been hard to deal with? How have you seen God at work for good in the midst of the suffering?
- What would you say if someone were to ask you, "If God really loves me, why do bad things happen to me?"
- Do you believe God is responsible for everything that happens? Why? Why not?
- What's the difference between good and bad people? Would you define yourself as good? Why, or why not?

(Additional questions on CD)

CLOSING (Handout on CD)

Serenity Prayer

God, grant me the serenity to accept the things I cannot change, courage to change the things I can, and the wisdom to know the difference, living one day at a time, enjoying one moment at a time, accepting hardship as a pathway to peace, taking, as Jesus did, this sinful world as it is, not as I would have it, trusting that you will make all things right if I surrender to your will, so that I may be reasonably happy in this life and supremely happy with you forever in the next. —Reinhold Niebuhr

GOD AND SCIENCE

SOUL FOOD: Science tells us about the creation; Scripture tells us about the Creator.

SCRIPTURE: Genesis 1 (Creation)

 **GAMES** (Additional game on CD)

Futurama

Ask your group members to come dressed in outfits they think will be worn in the future. (Make it clear that clothes are required.) Have a costume contest, and give a prize to the person with the best costume.

Long John Stuff

Buy some XXXL long johns. You will need enough to give a top and bottom to one person in each grade, team, or small group. Buy some nine-inch balloons. Ask for a volunteer from each grade, team, or small group. Hand out the long johns, and have the volunteers put them on over their clothes. Ask for two or three other volunteers from each group who can blow up and tie balloons. Give them the balloons. On "Go!" have them blow up and tie the balloons. Next they shove them inside the long johns worn by volunteer player Number 1. Play for 90 seconds. When time is up, take a pushpin and go to each person in long johns, pop the balloons one at a time using the pushpin. Count as you pop. The group with the most inflated balloons stuffed inside the long johns wins. (Try playing the girls first and then guys.)

 **SHARE AND CARE GROUPS**

Checking in: Highs and lows of the week, prayer requests, and prayer

 **Warm up:** What have you learned about evolution in school? What problems (if any) do you have with the theory of evolution? Do you think that science will ever prove or disprove God? Why? (Additional questions on CD)

FOCUS POINT (Additional idea on CD)

Video Option: *Contact* (1997) (Start 2:11:44; stop 2:17:39) Ellie testifies before a U.S. Senate committee after her incredible ride through space. She tells the committee that she could be wrong, but that what she saw and experienced has changed her forever. The clip ends as her limo drives away from the U.S. Capitol Building.

HAVE IT YOUR WAY!

Choose from, adapt, or rearrange these elements to create the best soul feast for your youth group.

THE FIXIN'S

More fun stuff to make the theme extra special! Your choice.

Munchies

Out of This World Pie

Popular Songs

Use these before and/or after the program to engage the youth. These are some options. Try to include the latest appropriate popular songs.

- "Evolution ... Redefined," by Geoff Moore (*Evolution*)
- "Chap Stick, Chapped Lips, and Things Like Chemistry," by Relient K (*Two Lefts Don't Make a Right ... But Three Do*)
- "Satellite," by Dave Matthews Band (*Under the Table and Dreaming*)
- "Satellite," by P.O.D. (*Satellite*)
- "It Is Well With My Soul/The River's Gonna Keep on Rolling," by Amy Grant (*Legacy Hymns & Faith*)

Worship and Praise Music

- "Lovely Noise," by Chrystina Lloree (*Faith*)
- "Wonderful Maker," by Chris Tomlin (*Not to Us*)
- "Potter's Hand," by Darlene Zschech (*Shout to the Lord 2000*)
- "Did You Feel the Mountains Tremble?" by Delirious (*Cutting Edge*)
- "Wonderful King," by David Crowder (*Can You Hear Us?*)
- "How Great Thou Art"

⊚ Other Movie Options

Choose one of these other movies, or ask students to recommend a more recent release. Be sure to preview your selection to avoid any content that would be objectionable in your setting. Remember that you must have a video license.
(Video licensing information on CD)

- *Planet of the Apes* (1968)
- *Hollow Man* (R) (2000)
- *Raiders of the Lost Ark* (1981)
- *Signs* (2002)
- *Jurassic Park* (1993)
- *King Kong* (1933 or 1976)
- *Blast From the Past* (1999)

Leader Scripture Exploration

- **Genesis 2** (The second Creation story)
- **Job 38:1-11** (God's mysteries)
- **Psalm 8** (The wonder of creation)
- **Psalm 104** (God creates.)

⊚ On Screen

Key points in Focus Thoughts (PowerPoint® on CD)

Leader Tip

Much of our society is biblically illiterate. Don't assume that all of your youth are familiar with this very well-known Creation story. Some may know it generally but may have never read it. Depending upon your group, you may wish to show them how to find it in the Bible and to tell them that the word *genesis* refers to "beginnings."

You may also need to deal with the fact that Genesis has two different Creation stories. While the order of creation differs, the message is still the same: God is the Creator. The biblical Creation stories are statements of faith.

Skit Option: Have volunteers dramatize the Creation story from **Genesis 1** while it's being read. Involve the rest of the group in repeating the line: "And there was evening and there was morning, the (particular) day."

⊚ FOCUS THOUGHTS  (Text and inserts on CD)

As recently as January 2004, the state school superintendent in Georgia proposed eliminating the word *evolution* from the state's science curriculum. The proposal was greeted with outrage by science teachers and academics; it was applauded by creationists and fundamentalist church goers. The controversy got plenty of ink on the pages of Georgia's newspapers, and one of the state's most famous Christians—former president Jimmy Carter—even voiced his opinion on the subject. (He was critical of the proposal.)

This recent hullabaloo over whether to teach the theory of evolution in public schools is evidence that science and religion—after centuries of tension and controversy—still have trouble getting along. In the early sixteenth century, Pope Paul V declared Galileo's astronomical discoveries and Copernicus's theory that the earth revolved around the sun heretical (contrary to the teachings of the church and Scripture). Many nineteenth-century Christians reacted harshly to the publication of Charles Darwin's "On the Origin of Species by Means of Natural Selection" in 1859.

The 1925 trial of Tennessee biology teacher John Scopes—who was charged with illegally teaching the theory of evolution—set the stage for an all-star debate between three-time presidential candidate, William Jennings Bryant, and renowned attorney, Clarence Darrow. The famous "Monkey Trial" was supposed to determine whether Tennessee's anti-evolution law was constitutional; but it quickly turned into a heated battle between science and faith, between Darwin's book and the Book of Genesis.

The battle continues today: "God versus science! Creation versus evolution! Two fighters enter the ring, but only one will emerge the champion. Who holds the truth about the mysteries of the universe?"

Hold on. Stop the fight. This is getting out of hand. If the Bible is true, must scientific theories such as the theory of evolution be false? If scientists were to prove true the theory of evolution, would the Bible lose its credibility?

According to many Christians, no. Not at all. Many individual Christians and Christian denominations feel that science complements their faith. Science is just one way of understanding how God works.

⊚ *(Add one or more of the underline examples from the CD if you'd like.)*

Science and Scripture have different objectives. Science seeks to understand how the universe works. Scripture tells us who created the universe and why this Creator is still at work. The opening chapters of Genesis, for example, tell us that God created all that is, that God created human beings in God's image, and that God seeks a relationship with God's human creations. Theories of evolution or the origin of the universe tell us how God may have brought everything into being and how humans may have developed into the complex creatures with whom God interacts.

Scripture tells us that, through Christ, God is working to redeem all of Creation. Science tells us how we can better care for God's creation and how we can use our God-given talents and resources to better care for one another. Why do we like to have science and religion fight with each other when they can work together so well?

As scientists further explore the vastness of the cosmos, the intricacies of subatomic quantum physics, and the complexities of the human body, Christians can further appreciate the magnitude and magnificence of God. Creation is full of mystery—some mysteries we will come to understand; others will remain beyond our comprehension.

What is important is that we recognize a) that this spectacular Creation is being carefully crafted by God, b) that all of God's creation has value, and c) that God has a purpose for what God has created. Likewise, each of us has been carefully crafted by God; each of us has value; and each of us was created with a purpose—a role to play in the ongoing story that God is writing. Let's pray.

Focus Groups

- How would you respond to a person who asked, "Why would any intelligent person believe in God? You can't prove that God exists."
- What makes it hard for some people to believe the Genesis Creation story?
- Do you think that evolution denies God? Why, or why not?
- Does it really matter—the whole evolution vs. creation controversy? Explain your answer.
- Respond to the following statement: There is no purpose to life if there is no Creator God.

(Additional questions on CD)

Closing

Slide Show

Invite a team of youth in advance to put together a slide show that illustrates the Scripture; they may also add music.

Litany of Praise

Have the group read this litany excerpted from Psalm 148. (Handout on CD)

Great Drumming

The Native American song "Many and Great, O God," found in some hymnals, can easily be sung to the beat of a drum or tom-tom.

Instead of a Message

Host a debate: Big Bang vs. God. (Instructions on CD)

On-the-Street Interviews

Have the youth videotape interviews with people on the following question: Which makes more sense: The Big Bang Theory, the Theory of Evolution, or God as the creator of everything?

Out and About

- Take your group to a planetarium. You can use this as a setting for your program and maybe enjoy a cool laser show at the same time.

- Go on a college campus tour or conduct your program in a local high school science lab.

- If you live near a desert, go there and have a guide point out the animals that inhabit the area that youth might not otherwise know about.

- Conduct worship outside. Invite everyone to use his or her senses to appreciate God's handiwork.

Music Video

"Psalm 139" (spoken), by Michael W. Smith (*Worship* video) (Ordering information on CD)

Scientist's Witness Statement

Invite a scientist who is also a Christian to talk about how his or her work has confirmed his or her faith. He or she may be able to use visual elements as part of the statement. (How-to on CD)

WHAT'S SO SPECIAL ABOUT JESUS?

HAVE IT YOUR WAY!

Choose from, adapt, or rearrange these elements to create the best soul feast for your youth group.

THE FIXIN'S

More fun stuff to make the theme extra special! Your choice.

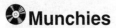Munchies

Contact a local chef in your area to visit your group and prepare some awesome desserts. (If you do this during your talk, your room will smell great and the youth will definitely want to hang around for a social time.) Have him or her describe the process. What makes each desert so special? To save time, some desserts can already be prepared. Enjoy!

Popular Songs

Use these before and/or after the program to engage the youth. These are some options. Try to include the latest appropriate popular songs.

- "God So Loved," by Jaci Velasquez (*Jaci*)
- "One of Us," by Joan Osborne (*Relish*)
- "Show Me the Way," by Styx (*Styx—Greatest Hits*)
- "With Arms Wide Open," by Creed (*Human Clay*)
- "You Are the Way," by True Vibe (*True Vibe*)

SOUL FOOD: When we get to know Jesus, we discover God's Son, beckoning us to follow him.

SCRIPTURE: Matthew 16:14-16 (Who do you say I am?)

Games

I Have/I Have Not

Tell your group members to gather chairs and form a circle. One person stands in the middle. This person will say, "I have _____." Anyone in the circle who also has _____ gets up and runs to another chair at least two chairs away. The person who is left without a chair is the person to say, "I have _____." Change the game after a few minutes to I Have Not. The person in the middle simply says, "I have not _____." People in the circle who have not _____ must move chairs. This is an old game but is wild fun.

Something Special

Create your own youth group holiday. What is special about your group? Plaster your logo on everything. Have a used gift exchange (don't forget old youth group t-shirts). Create a celebration song and rituals (candles, dances, chants). Have the youth perform skits to highlight their favorite youth group memories. This can become a tradition each year. You might choose to have it a few weeks after school begins.

SHARE AND CARE GROUPS

Checking in: Highs and lows of the week, prayer requests, and prayer

Warm up: What has been your experience with people of religions other than Christianity? Why is it important to live what you believe? How do you express your faith outside the church building? How do you express your faith at school? How does living your faith affect your friends? Does it? (Additional questions on CD)

FOCUS POINT

Video Option: *Veggie Tales—An Easter Carol* (2004) (Start 30:31; stop 34:15) This clip includes a song that tells the story of the life of Jesus.

On-the-Street Interviews Option: Ask people to describe Jesus. Ask them to identify the difference between Jesus and other religious leaders. Videotape their answers.

FOCUS THOUGHTS (Text and quizzes on CD)

What's so special about Jesus? If I asked that question to each of you, I am sure that we would have lots of different answers. In **Matthew 16:14-16,** Jesus asked his closest friends what people were saying about him: "Some say John the Baptist, but others Elijah, still others Jeremiah or one of the prophets." Then Jesus asked the disciples who they thought he was. "Simon Peter answered, "You are the Messiah, the Son of the loving God."

All but one of the disciples was murdered for what they believed about Jesus. JESUS: What you think about him—what you believe—really matters. Your answer has eternal consequences.

Legally, in the United States, all religions are on the same level. Some people believe that all religions point to the same God. But let's look at some differences.

(For the sake of simplicity, we will not use in our comparison either Hinduism or Judaism. Hinduism—because it has no central leader and lots of gods; Judaism—because it has a special place in our own Christian faith.)

Help me out with the answers as we go. (PowerPoint®quizzes on CD)

Jesus fulfilled many prophecies, taught people how be loving, performed miracles, lived a perfectly moral life, died, rose from the grave, and appeared to many very much alive and well. He ascended into heaven with a promise to be with us always.

For 2,000 years people have called him "Savior and Lord" and had their lives changed for the better.

SO WHAT DO YOU THINK? What's so special about Jesus? Jesus, the Son of God, invites you to follow him and discover for yourself!

Your answer will change your life today and forever. Let's pray.

FOCUS GROUP (Additional questions on CD)

- Who is Jesus to you? Teacher? Prophet? Doctor? Son of God? Crazy man?
- What are your thoughts on the following statement: All religions lead to the same God? If that is a true statement, why do you think Jesus had to die for Christians? (No other major religious leaders had to die for their followers.) Why do you think God went to such extremes to prove love and show forgiveness?
- What does it mean to accept Jesus as Savior and Lord?
- How has being a follower of Jesus Christ affected your life?
- As believers in Jesus, how should we treat persons who have different beliefs?

Worship and Praise Music

- "Holy and Anointed One," by Randy Butler (*WOW Worship Orange—Today's 30 Most Powerful Worship Songs*)
- "My Redeemer Lives," by Hillsongs Australia (*Shout to the Lord 2000*)
- "Raise Up the Crown (All Hail the Power of Jesus' Name)," by Passion Worship Band (*Hymns Ancient and Modern: Live Songs of Our Faith*)

Other Movie Options

Choose one of these other movies, or ask students to recommend a more recent release. Be sure to preview your selection to avoid any content that would be objectionable in your setting. Remember that you must have a video license.
(Video licensing information on CD)

- *The Passion of the Christ* (R) (2004)
- *Armageddon* (1998)
- *Dances With Wolves* (1990)
- *The Natural* (1984)
- *Driving Miss Daisy* (1990)

On Screen

Quizzes for Focus Thoughts (PowerPoint® on CD)

Leader Scripture Exploration

Luke 1:26–2:20 (Jesus is born.)
Mark 6:45-51 (Jesus calms the storm.)
1 Peter 2:4-8 (Jesus is the cornerstone.)
Matthew 27:62–28:15 (Jesus is resurrected.)

Instead of a Message

Host a Debate: Divide the youth into at least three groups. Have one group research Jesus. Have another research Buddha. Have the remaining group research Mohammed. Have a debate to see whether your group can discover who should be believed. Read through the Focus Thoughts and quizzes to sharpen your knowledge. Be prepared to add any insights you learn that the groups do not bring up. Don't forget to forewarn your pastor. This subject can be touchy for some parents.

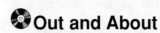Out and About

Visit the worship center of a different faith, such as a Jewish synagogue. Most are more than happy to welcome an inquisitive group of youth. Be confident in your students to allow them to see and hear from others. (Additional idea on CD)

Youth Witness Statement

Invite a youth to tell about something that he or she did or said that had an impact upon a person in such a way that he or she became a Christ follower or grew stronger in faith.

Or invite a youth to tell about an experience of being persecuted for his or her faith. (How-to on CD) (Sample witness statement on CD)

Closing

Song Fest

Now is a good time to use the musical testimonies of the ages. Bring out the hymnals, songbooks, and big-screen lyrics. Prompt your best song leaders, singers, musicians to be prepared to raise the roof in praise! Spend this worship time singing about Jesus. Add a solo or two, as well. Use songs such as these (first verses for most):

"O How I Love Jesus"
"There's Something About That Name"
"Majesty, Worship His Majesty"
"Fairest Lord Jesus"
"Jesus Loves Me"
"Lord, I Lift Your Name on High"
"Lord of the Dance"
"He Lives"
"In the Garden"
"I Love to Tell the Story"

Lift High the Cross

If your church has large cross that can be carried, or you can make one, have a youth bring it forward in a procession as the group sings the chorus to "Lift High the Cross" several times. Close with a sending forth that builds on the experience of the meeting—discovering Jesus, who loved us so much that he would die for our sin, following Jesus who calls us to love others, sharing Jesus with a hurting world.

Now What?

Give the youth information about becoming and growing as a Christian. Make available the booklet *Now What? Next Steps for Your New Life in Christ* (Information on CD).

Or invite youth to take a copy of "Would You Like to Connect With God?" (Handout on CD), which highlights the basics of committing their lives to God.

can THIS Really Make a DIFFeReNce in MY LiFe?

SOUL FOOD: When we open our hearts to God, we gain more than we can imagine.

SCRIPTURE: Psalm 119:1-3 (Happy are those who seek God and walk with God.)

 **Games** (Additional game on CD)

Quick Change Artists

Have the youth find a partner and stand face to face. Then have them turn and stand back-to-back. Have them change something about their appearance. Have them turn back around and try to identify the change in ten seconds or less.

Bible Skits

In advance, ask four or five youth to create a short skit to tell the story of a person in the Bible. The centurion at the cross, Peter, Thomas, Paul, and the woman at the well are all good ones to dramatize. Ask them to focus on how belief in Christ changed the life of the person. Encourage them to create a costume for their character.

 **SHARE AND CARE GROUPS**

Checking in: Highs and lows of the week, prayer requests, and prayer

 Warm up: Tell about someone you know who is like Jesus. What do you tell a friend who asks, "If I take the time to believe, will it help me in my life?" Have you ever thought, *In such a big world, with so many people, how can God hear my prayers or make a difference in my life?* (Additional questions on CD)

FOCUS POINT

Video Option: *Hope Floats* (1998) (Start 31:45; stop 34:35) Birdee runs into an old classmate who has changed significantly. Birdee apologizes for how she treated Dot and asks for her forgiveness.

Have It Your Way!

Choose from, adapt, or rearrange these elements to create the best soul feast for your youth group.

THE FIXIN'S

More fun stuff to make the theme extra special! Your choice.

Munchies

Have foods that are made better by adding something: apple pie with homemade whipped cream, ice cream with chocolate syrup, chocolate covered strawberries, and so forth.

Popular Songs

Use these before and/or after the program to engage the youth. These are some options. Try to include the latest appropriate popular songs.

- "Little Miss Magic," by Jimmy Buffett (*Coconut Telegraph*)
- "I'm a Believer," by Smash Mouth (*Shrek—Music From the Original Motion Picture*)
- "We Will Rock You," by Queen (*Queen—Greatest Hits*)

Worship and Praise Music

- "I Could Sing of Your Love Forever," by SonicFlood (*Worship Together: I Could Sing of Your Love Forever*)
- "Refiner's Fire," by Brian Doerksen (*25 Top Vineyard Worship Songs: Draw Me Close*)
- "Enough," Chris Tomlin (*Not to Us*)
- "My Glorious," by Delirious (*Touch*)
- "Get Down," by Audio Adrenaline (*Underdog*)

Other Movie Options

Choose one of these movies, or ask students to recommend a more recent release. Be sure to preview your selection to avoid any content that would be objectionable in your setting. Remember that you must have a video license.
(Video licensing information on CD)

• *Nell* (1994)
• *Dead Poets Society* (1989)
• *About a Boy* (2002)

On-the-Street Interviews

Have the youth videotape interviews where they ask random people to tell about a time when their belief in God made a difference in their lives.

Leader Scripture Exploration

Isaiah 30:20-21 (God directs the path of followers.)
Jeremiah 29:11-14a (God has good plans for believers.)
Romans 12:1-2 (Walk according to God's will.)

 On Screen

Today's Scripture, **Psalm 119:1-3**
(PowerPoint® on CD)

Instead of a Message

Intergenerational Sharing: Have a time when people of various ages can tell what God is doing in their lives.
(More on CD)

Scripture Presentation: (PowerPoint®on CD) Invite two youth to do a brief skit focusing on the question, "Will I ever be happy?"and dramatic reading of **Psalm 119:1-3** (Happy are those who seek God and walk with God).

Focus Thoughts (Text on CD)

This Witness Statement was made by Clinton Adams, a high school senior from Peachtree City, Georgia. Read it or have a student read it aloud as if speaking. Or better yet, find a youth in your group who can make a similar personal testimony for this program's Focus Thoughts.

I've grown up as the shy, nice guy. I have had a good core group of friends my entire life. I never got into trouble, and I've made good-enough grades. What could be better than that? However, for some reason I was never a real happy kid. I wasn't dreary, but I wasn't happy or content with life. There just had to be some point to life that I didn't know of.

During my freshman year in high school, my best friends invited me to come to this cool youth group for a white-water rafting trip. I then decided to give the regular youth group activities a try. The Sunday night activities were fun, but nothing really had an affect on me.

Fast-forward about three months and I found myself on a trip called Spiritual Life Advance. On the last night we opened "Love Letters" that our parents had written to us. We followed that with the most moving prayer exercise I had ever seen. That night I opened my heart to God for the first time.

What really made the difference in my experience was that I followed up this trip with spiritual conversations with my friends and I started serving others and God through the youth group. A few months later I started to have deep talks with our youth director; those talks have been a catalyst in my spiritual growth. I have also had other experiences that have had a dramatic impact on my life. My first big retreat was amazing—1,500 kids, all worshiping God! There were awesome speakers and a great band too. The whole week is one life-changing event after another.

Another life-changing event was our mission trip to Chile. I went into the trip thinking we would be helping other people. I came out of it having learned and experienced much more than I could ever give. It was truly a blessing to see these people, who only own the bare essentials of life, be so happy with their life and relationship with God. I learned you only need God to live—nothing else is required.

Since I have accepted God into my heart, I have had a different outlook on life! Now I have a purpose: to serve Jesus Christ in everything I do, even if it's only sweeping the floor!

Focus Group

• Tell the group about someone who has had his or her life changed because of faith in God.
• How has having faith made a difference in your life? Are there small things you may be overlooking?

- What would life look like if you were a fully devoted follower of Christ?
- Are you willing to give God a chance for the next month to see whether that decision really makes a difference?

(Additional questions on CD)

CLOSING

Ritual of Remembrance

Round up your group into a circle sitting on the floor. Turn off the lights and light one candle. Have each person tell about someone who has had a significant impact on him or her. Older adults, parents, teachers, friends—ask the youth to concentrate on those people who made an impact on their faith.

Go Beyond Belief to Action

Use your small groups for the following closing. Give each student two sheets of construction paper. Supply each group with scissors and markers. Ask the youth to outline their shoes on the sheets of paper. Then instruct them to cut out their prints.

Encourage group members to consider how they will take their faith beyond belief to action. What can they do each day to show that they believe? at home? at School? at work? at practice? on a date? How can they help reveal God's kingdom on earth? Ask them to write their answers on their footprints.

Invite them to tell some of their answers to their group. It is OK not to share things that are very personal.

Sending Forth (Handout on CD)

Assign readers according to the handout. Encourage reading with a dramatic flair.

> We were not there in the beginning when God said, "Let there be light!" and there was! There was land, life, and people like us. It seems so long ago. It seems so hard to believe.
>
> We were not there with the disciples—two feet from God—as Jesus was serving—washing feet, raising the dead, healing the lame and blind. We were not there to see him. We were not there to hear the words from his mouth. It was hard for those two feet away to believe—how much harder it is for us!
>
> Oh, to be two feet from God today, watching as lives are transformed, experiencing true unconditional love, being made whole from the inside out, living in the paradise that was part of the original plan. If only we could see God!
>
> Look up! Look around! You *are* two feet from God. Jesus is at work around you, in you, and through you.
>
> Open your eyes and see! God is here! Open your ears and hear! God is here! Open your heart to love and be loved. God is here! Open your self to God. God is here!

Service Projects

- Have your group members sign up to do a service project each week in their own homes. Parents won't believe it. This commitment should not include regular chores but should be unexpected tasks such as cleaning the oven, scrubbing the bathroom floors, cleaning the baseboards, washing the windows and doing extra yard work.

- Set up an international mission trip. (More on CD)

Special

Take a girl and a guy from your group and give them a Saturday makeover. You might ask their parents to help pay for the haircut. Ask your volunteers to chip in some money for some new clothes. You might even start a few weeks early by placing six buckets out on a table with the names of youth volunteers on them. Have the group donate change to see who should receive the makeover. Use this money for the treat. One catch: The winners must agree to be the youth group servants for the next month. In the program, compare and contrast the physical, external change and its results with the internal change that Christ brings about, making a "new creation" (2 Corinthians 5:17).

Rescue 9-1-1

HeLP! HeLP!

We all experience times in our lives when we need help. We can't do it, make it, survive it on our own. Humans are connected to one another. We need to be rescued, and we need to help rescue others.

Sometimes we even need to be rescued from ourselves. It's easy to let sin turn the limelight on ourselves at the expense of others or the natural world. Only God can rescue us from the power of sin to a life powered by love.

APPetizers

Publicity Ideas: *Don't neglect advertising (within your church and elsewhere). Use your imagination. Create a timeline for maximum effect. Spread the word with passion.*

- Create a flyer using the theme logo from the CD; include dates, times, and location. Advertise in your church bulletin, in your youth newsletter, and on posters around the church.

- Borrow a firefighter's coat and hat; deliver flyers with the program information on it in person to members of your group. Give them an extra flyer to give to a friend.

- Use the firefighter's coat and hat; come into worship service at announcement time, "looking for someone to rescue." (Make sure that the pastor knows about the plan in advance.)

- Do an e-mail blast. Send the e-mails to the youth; ask the youth to forward the e-mails to their friends too. Use the theme logo as part of the blast.

- Use flashing emergency lights after worship service to call attention to the theme for youth group.

- Find out whether you know anyone who has a St. Bernard dog or another type of search-and-rescue dog. If someone has one, find a way to use the animal in your publicity.

- Create a skit with a rescue theme. Video tape it, and show it during announcement time as a preview of what's coming. Make and give copies of the video to your youth. Encourage them to give their copy to a friend along with an invitation to come to the series.

COMBOS MENU

Main Dishes

Weekly Program Options: *Choose one or all; do in any order. Check each description for the fixin's.*

1. **The Chief Firefighter**—Many people think of religion in terms of heaven and hell. Youth often have questions about "going to hell." Here's an opportunity to look both at the reality of hell and at the love of God, who rescues us from it.

2. **EMT**—Life happens! People get wounded. People are hurting. God calls us to be first-responders, to help rescue and heal—especially those right at our "gates."

3. **Forest Ranger**—Sometimes people act as though we're the only ones on earth, and everything is for our use and pleasure. But listen closely: The critters, the land, the water, the air are calling, "Rescue me!"

4. **Justice of the Peace**—"Yes, but ... I'm not Superman. I can't do anything to right the wrongs of the world!" Look again at the lowly justice of the peace. You do have power to rescue people from injustice.

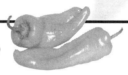

Spice It Up

Theme Decorations: *Look at your space. Use your imagination. Give away or auction off purchased decorations as prizes at the end of the week or the theme.*

- Use flashing emergency lights at strategic locations. Check at the automotive section of a large discount store to find the lights.

- Put together or borrow a "highway safety" kit.

- Check with the Red Cross for big posters and a sample disaster relief kit.

- Add yellow caution zone tape, fire station garb, climbing gear, a stretcher, life preserver, pictures of St. Bernards, and so forth.

- Raid the Halloween costume stash for firefighter and super hero costumes, hats, and gear.

- Recreate an ambulance or firetruck look.

- Use red, orange, and yellow paper, crepe paper, or cellophane to make the learning area look like "hell."

Drinks

" 'Lord, when was it that we saw you ... thirsty and gave you something to drink? ...' 'Truly, I tell you, just as you did it to one of the least of these' " (Matthew 25:37, 40a).

Service project ideas

CHIEF FIREFIGHTER

HaVe It Your Way!

Choose from, adapt, or rearrange these elements to create the best soul feast for your youth group.

The Fixin's

More fun stuff to make the theme extra special! Your choice.

Munchies

- Devil's Food Cake
- Angel Food Cake
- Red Hots (candy)

Popular Songs

Use these before and/or after the program to engage the youth. These are some options. Try to include the latest appropriate popular songs.

- "Hell," by the Squirrel Nut Zippers (*Hot*)
- "Burning Down the House," by the Talking Heads (*The Best of the Talking Heads*)
- "Rescue Me" by Fontella Bass (*Sister Act*)
- "You Cannot Lose My Love," by Sara Groves (*All Right Here*)

Worship and Praise Music

- "Consuming Fire," by Third Day (*Offerings: A Worship Album*)
- "King of the Jungle," by Steven Curtis Chapmann (*Heaven in the Real World*)
- "Enough," by Chris Tomlin (*Not to Us*)
- "Lord, I Lift Your Name on High," by SonicFlood (*Worship Together: I Could Sing of Your Love Forever*)

Announcements

Use a megaphone.

SOUL FOOD: Jesus Christ can rescue us from the hell of being separated from God, who loves us.

SCRIPTURE: John 3:16-17 (God sent God's own Son); Romans 6:23 (The free gift of God)

 Games

Spider Web (Construction information on CD)

Construct a "web" about 10 feet wide by 7 feet high. Leave holes large enough for a person to pass through. The challenge is to get the team through the web, using only their bodies. They'll need to work together.

Hell Tag

This game plays like regular tag but with a dark twist. Before the game write the word *angel* on 3–5 small slips of paper. On 3–5 more slips write *darkside agent*. The rest of the game is played just like tag. If someone is tagged by a darkside agent, he or she must go to "hell." The angels can save a person from hell by circling the people in hell and singing the first verse of "Amazing Grace." For each successful completion of the verse without getting tagged, one person is freed. Call time and decide the winners.

Share and Care Groups

Checking in: Highs and lows of the week, prayer requests, and prayer

Warm up: Have you ever been around a major fire? What was it like? How have you heard "hell" described? Do you tend to do things because you are afraid of punishment or because you see real benefit in doing it? Which is more motivating to you?

Focus Point

Video Options: *Little Nicky* (2000) (Start 2:53—A man is falling into hell; stop 3:45—the tower abode of the devil). Preview this segment carefully. We recommend that you keep the sound off. Play loud "hellish" sound effects instead.

Art Option: Set out the art supplies and invite the youth to create various interpretations of what hell might be like. They may go traditional (with flames and devilish characters), create a spoof (something that would feel like hell, for example, listening to little kids' TV songs for eternity); depict "hell on earth" (perhaps a person experiencing the despair of being absent from God).

⊙FOCUS THOUGHTS (Text on CD)

Hell! Let's talk about hell. Undoubtedly, you have some ideas of what hell is supposed to be like—fiery torture that never ends. That image is truly part of our Christian heritage. Some Christians (perhaps even some of your friends) belong to churches that really stress the idea that if you don't do right, you will go to hell. (We'll talk more about that next week.)

For now, let's look at where that idea comes from. In much of the Old Testament, *Sheol* was named as the place of the dead. It held neither punishment nor reward; it was simply the place where the dead would continue to exist. It was located under the earth. (That idea was way before people discovered that the earth was round.)

In King David's time, Gehenna, a valley south of Jerusalem, was where a cult of people following a foreign god made burnt offerings of children. Eventually, it became the place where the people of Jerusalem burned their garbage and the bodies of people who had no burial place. Gehenna's history of fire and burning bodies provided a dominant image for what we call hell.

You may ask, Is hell a real place or just an image? That question misses the point:

- Hell is a reality but not necessarily a specific or actual place. Rather, the reality is that we can separate ourselves from God. Being alienated from the One who loves us is hell.

- Hell is a reality but not exclusively a future consequence. People separated from God and alienated from one another experience hell now, a "hell on earth."

Who can save us from hell? Only God can. Let's look at a very familiar passage of Scripture. (*Read aloud* **John 3:16-17.**)

God sent the "Chief Firefighter" so that we would not perish, but be saved. God sent God's own Son Jesus Christ to bridge the separation and make it possible for us to have eternal life.

It's easy to think of "eternal life" and hell as out there in the future, but God's offer is life—now and always—in God's presence.

What do we know about God? Why would we want to be in God's presence now and always?

- God loves the world—you and me, included.
- God loves us so much that God has given God's own Son for us.
- God does not want the world to be condemned.
- God wants good for us—now and always.

Why would we *not* want to be in the presence of such love—now and always?

But God gives us a choice. (*Read aloud* **Romans 6:23.**) Life apart from God is hell. It's filled with sin and death, but God's offer of life with God is a free gift. We make the choice. Jesus Christ is our chief firefighter, ready to save us. We need simply to open our hearts and allow him to rescue us.

Let's pray.

⊙Other Movie Options

Choose one of these movies, or ask students to recommend a more recent release. Be sure to preview your selection to avoid any content that would be objectionable in your setting. Remember that you must have a video license. (Video licensing information on CD)

- *Bill and Ted's Bogus Journey* (1991)
- *Hell House* (2001) (*For more information visit www.culturevulture.net/Movies5/ HellHouse.htm OR www.hellhousemovie.com*)

Leader Scripture Exploration

- **John 3:1-21** (Nicodemus comes by night.)
- **John 7:45-52** (Nicodemus is sympathetic toward Jesus' message.)
- **John 19:38-42** (Nicodemus shows his love for Jesus Christ)

⊙On Screen

Key points from Focus Thoughts (PowerPoint® and Text on CD)

Create a Video

Create a skit in which the main character is completely ignored by everyone. Follow with a discussion of what it must have felt like for the person ignored.

⊙Instead of a Message

Read aloud "Heaven and Hell," from *Stories for Telling: A Treasury for Christian Storytellers*, by William R. White (Augsburg Fortress, 1986; ISBN: 0806621923) (Ordering information on CD)

Out and About

- Visit a fire station.

- If it's Halloween time, visit a "haunted house." Be sure to debrief the experience. If you visit a "Hell House," allow lots of time for preparation and discussion afterward. Also talk about what a "Grace House" would look like.

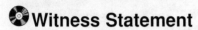

Witness Statement

Invite a youth or an adult to tell about his or her experience of "hell on earth" and how he or she experienced being rescued.
(How-to on CD)

Posters

Jesus loves the hell out of you!
(Design on CD)

I don't live in fear of Hell; I live in praise of God! (Design on CD)

FOCUS GROUP

- How have you thought of hell in the past? What do you think about it now?
- What kinds of conversations have you had with your friends about heaven and hell?
- Do you think that God is trying to scare us into being good?
- What would you tell someone about what God is like?

CLOSING

God's Chief Firefighter

Gather the group in the sanctuary or at your worship space. Darken the room, with only a few candles for light. At the end of the meditation, play soft music and allow the youth to leave individually.

Nicodemus was curious about Jesus; but he was Pharisee, and his Pharisee buddies were all abuzz about how crazy-wrong this Jesus was. Peer pressure kept Nicodemus away. But when it was dark and his buddies weren't likely to see him, Nicodemus went to Jesus.

The conversation was confusing to Nick. Jesus was talking about being "born from above, born of water and Spirit." *How can that be?* he wondered aloud. It was in that explanation that Jesus said these most famous words of **John 3:16:**

> "For God so loved the world that he gave his only Son, so that everyone who believes in him may not perish but may have eternal life."

Nicodemus didn't have the benefit of the whole New Testament, nor the witness of 2,000 years of Christians that we do to help him understand what it means to be born again, to be born through the Spirit. But he encountered the living Christ, and his life was changed.

We too can be born again through the Holy Spirit, born again into a new relationship with the God who loves us. God sent God's own Son to rescue us from the power of sin and death and to bring us into God's loving presence—now and always!

For those of you who have not knelt before this loving God and given back your heart, mind, soul, and strength in thanksgiving, I invite you to make that commitment now at the altar. Come; stay and pray as long as you like.

For those of you who know the joy of being rescued by God's Chief Firefighter, who know the love of Jesus personally, I invite you to come to the altar also. Come, pray for those who do not yet know that Jesus is ready to rescue them too! Stay and pray as long as you choose; leave quietly when you are ready.

EMT

SOUL FOOD: Christians are called to care for the wounded of the world.

SCRIPTURE: Luke 16:19-31 (The rich man and Lazarus)

Games

Rescue Races

Two people carry a third person, who pretends to be unconscious or to have a broken leg (you assign the problem). Or two people carry a third person on a stretcher. Have teams compete to finish the prescribed course. Increase the excitement by doing the race as a relay competition.

Bandage Wrap Relay

Teams have an equal number of elastic and cloth bandages and race to bandage one of their members until they are out of bandages. Add a fun twist by making the wrapped person walk ten feet to make sure the wraps will stay on.

SHARE AND CARE GROUPS

Checking in: Highs and lows of the week, prayer requests, and prayer

Warm up: Have you ever observed or been involved in a rescue situation? Tell about it. What was the most recent situation you saw in life or on TV of people who were suffering? How were others responding to the need?

Video Option: *Radio* (2003) (Start 2:45; stop 4:52). Radio goes through town shunned, stared at, and yelled at. He is outside the gates of the football field; the coach notices him. This movie is an excellent one to show in its entirety. Host a movie night before or after this program to help youth make connections.

Scripture Option: Do a dramatic reading using several voices for each of the characters: Jesus as storyteller, the rich man, Abraham, and silent Lazarus. This passage lends itself to using multiple senses. See "Tormented in the Flame," from *Worship Feast Ideas*, page 64. (<u>Information on CD</u>)

HaVe It YOUR WaY!

Choose from, adapt, or rearrange these elements to create the best soul feast for your youth group.

THe FiXin'S

More fun stuff to make the theme extra special! Your choice.

Munchies

• Fireball candies and water
• Chips and hot salsa

Popular Songs

Use these before and/or after the program to engage the youth. These are some options. Try to include the latest appropriate popular songs.

• "We Are the World," by USA for Africa (*We Are the World*)
• "Lean on Me," by Bill Withers (*Bill Withers—Greatest Hits*)
• "Theme From ER," by James Newton-Howard (*ER: Original Television Theme Music and Score*)

Worship and Praise Music

• "Fix Me, Jesus"
• "To the Ends of the Earth," by Hillsongs (*Hope*)
• "Here I Am, Lord"
• "Holiness (Take My Life)," by SonicFlood (*Worship Together: Be Glorified*)
• "Give Us Clean Hands," by Chris Tomlin (*Worship Together: Be Glorified*)
• "They'll Know We Are Christians by Our Love"

⊙ Other Movie Options

Choose one of these movies, or ask students to recommend a more recent release. Be sure to preview your selection to avoid any content that would be objectionable in your setting. Remember that you must have a video license.
(Video licensing information on CD)

• *Patch Adams* (1998)
• *Pay It Forward* (2000)

Leader Exploration Scriptures

• **Exodus 3–4** (God calls Moses.)
• **Matthew 7:15-20** (Good trees bear good fruit.)
• **Matthew 13:36-43** (Jesus explains the parable of the weeds.)
• **Matthew 25:31-46** (The nations will be judged.)

⊙ Instead of a Message

Invite one or more guest speakers. Choose from relief workers, the Red Cross, a local shelter, or other community services.
(Suggestions for speakers on CD)

⊙ On Screen

Images of the wounded of the world for Focus Thoughts
(PowerPoint® and Text on CD)

⊙ FOCUS THOUGHTS (Text on CD)

Let me tell you a story. (*If you did not use the Scripture Option in Focus Point, read aloud* **Luke 16:19-31.**)

In the story, the rich man was in Hades, another word for hell. Obviously, he didn't do right and consequently went to hell. That fits with what we hear from some of our Christian brothers and sisters. But let's dig a little deeper.

Let's talk about Lazarus first. What do we know about him? He was poor, covered with sores, and hungry. *And* he was right outside the gate of the rich man's home. While he suffered in his lifetime, he was ultimately comforted.

• Who are the poor, the hurting, the hungry who are right outside our gates?

The rich man finally figured out that the way he had lived had brought him to eternal torture. He was struck with a flurry of compassion—not for Lazarus (notice that he wanted Lazarus to bring him a drink)—but for his "brothers" (the people who were like him, the people he liked to be with). Send someone to warn them, he begged.

• Isn't it much easier for us to be kind and compassionate to people who are like us?

Showing compassion is usually a good thing in the Bible, but here we have a surprise. Father Abraham (the one with whom God first made covenant) chided the rich man: They already have Moses and the prophets. (That's another way of saying that they should already know through the law and the words of God's spokespersons in the Scriptures what's important).

Father Abraham even pointed out that if someone were to come back from the dead, those guys most likely still wouldn't get it. I wonder how Jesus must have felt as he told this story. He must have felt sad, knowing that many people simply wouldn't "get" the Resurrection.

So what does this story say to us? If you don't do right, you'll go to hell—that's one way to look at it. But let's go back to what we know about God:

1. God loves all of us, including the Lazaruses of this world.

2. God has told us through the law and the prophets (and through Jesus himself) that God's vision for the world is not suffering—but healing and wholeness.

God is calling us to join the EMT—God's emergency medical team—to care for the wounded of the world, especially those who are right in front of us.

(*Show the PowerPoint® presentation.*)

It's our turn to be rescuers—not because we're afraid we'll go to hell, but because we ourselves have been rescued by Jesus Christ. We love because God first loved us.

Let's pray.

FOCUS GROUP (Alternative Bible study on CD)

- Who are the poor, the hurting, the hungry who are right outside our "gates"?
- How do most people respond to them? Why?
- What stops people from being kind and compassionate?
- Why is it much easier for us to be kind and compassionate to people who are like us? What barriers do we have to get over?
- How can we help one another be kind and compassionate?
- What do you think God is like?

CLOSING

God's EMT (Script on CD)

Do this closing as a drama; it's based on Exodus 3–4. Create a "burning bush" (Instructions on CD); and have God speak from out of sight, using a microphone if needed.

(Moses is casually walking by. The bush begins to blaze. He comes closer.)

God: Moses! Moses!

Moses: Here I am.

God: Take off your sandals; you are on holy ground. *(Moses complies.)*

God: I have seen the misery of my people; I have heard their cry under their taskmasters. Indeed, I know their sufferings; and I have come down to deliver them. I will send you.

Moses: Who am I to do this? I'm a nobody. I can't do this.

God: I will be with you.

Moses: I'm not a persuasive speaker. Sometimes I stutter; sometimes I just go blank.

God: Who gives speech to mortals? I do! Now go, and I will be with you and teach you what to say.

Moses: Please send someone else! I don't think I can do it.

God: I will send your brother Aaron to go with you. And I will be with you. *(Moses falls on his knees in prayer and then during the closing song rises confidently and strides forth.)*

Narrator: The wounded of this world are many. Some are in far-off lands; some are right outside our doors. God is calling us to be the church, to be part of God's EMT and care for those who are hurting. Like Moses, we may not feel up to the task; but God has given us one another and promises to be with us, teaching us what to do and say.

All: *(Sing "Here I Am, Lord.")*

Out and About

- Visit a Red Cross or other relief agency.

Service Projects

- Have the group help prepare and serve a meal at a soup kitchen. Talk before or afterward with the staff about the causes and cures for hunger.

- Do a clothing drive in your church and neighborhood. Collect and donate clean, usable clothing to a local center or to one that sends clothing to other countries. Have the group volunteer to help sort the clothing at the facility as well.

- Have the group prepare health kits or school kits to be distributed in areas of need. (Information on CD)

- Have the group sponsor a child, committing to at least one year. Most sponsorships are in the range of $25–$35 dollars per month. Contact *www.planusa.org* or *www.compassion.com*. Have two or three youth do the research and make a presentation to the group. Have the youth follow up periodically by writing letters to the sponsored child. These agencies also have project sponsorships available for a one-time donation.

Forest Rangers

Have It Your Way!
Choose from, adapt, or rearrange these elements to create the best soul feast for your youth group.

The Fixin's
More fun stuff to make the theme extra special! Your choice.

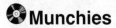 ### Munchies
- Animal Crackers
- Ants on a Log
- Organic foods
- Chocolate Mice

Add Parents
Make this a "Bring Your Parents Program." Engage parents in the whole program. Also take time to have families focus on what they can do together at home to care for the environment.

Popular Songs
Use these before and/or after the program to engage the youth. These are some options. Try to include the latest appropriate popular songs.

- "Big Yellow Taxi," by Counting Crows (*Films About Ghosts*)
- "Beautiful Day," by U2 (*All That You Can't Leave Behind*)
- "Stand," by R.E.M. (*Green*)
- "If a Tree Falls," by Bruce Cockburn (*Anything Anytime Anywhere: Singles 1979–2002*)

Worship and Praise Music
- "For the Beauty of the Earth"
- "All Things Bright and Beautiful"
- "How Great Thou Art"
- "God of the Sparrow, God of the Whale"

SOUL FOOD: God has given us the job of caring for, protecting, rescuing every living thing and the earth itself.

SCRIPTURE: Genesis 1:26-28 (The sixth day of Creation)

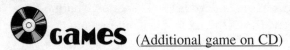 ## Games (Additional game on CD)

Recycle Races
Have each team line up behind a bag of recyclable items: clean aluminum or steel cans (make sure that there are no sharp edges), plastic containers (#1 or #2 only), newspapers, cardboard pieces. Each bag contains the same number and kinds of recyclables. The first person in line puts on a blindfold and then picks one item from the bag. He or she must race to the appropriate recycle bin, put the item in, get back to the team, and hand off the blindfold to the next person in line. Team members may yell directions to their recycler. The first team to empty its bag wins.

Snowstorm
Divide the youth into two teams. The teams will face each other, with a dividing line between. Give each team an equal stack of newspapers. For three minutes, each group tries to get as many newspaper wads across the line onto their opponent's side while keeping their side free of papers. No one is allowed to step over the line. At the end of time, gather the papers and be sure to take them for recycling.

SHARE AND CARE GROUPS
Checking in: Highs and lows of the week, prayer requests, and prayer

Warm up: What does your family recycle? (Think also of actions at home, such as reusing butter tubs to keep leftovers in, passing along clothing, donating older model cell phones.)

FOCUS POINT
Video Option: *Dr. Doolittle 2* (Start 17:17 with the beaver's speech; stop 19:06 with the squirrel's statement.)

Enviro-Quiz Option: Have the youth form teams of three or four, with every team having the same number. Read the question and give the teams a time limit to come up with their answer. Either have them number a paper

1–5 and choose their best answer (most correct answers wins), or play competitively (first correct answer from a team wins). Award prizes. (Quiz questions on CD)

⊙FOCUS THOUGHTS (Text on CD)

I love watching the Animal Planet channel on TV. I howl with laughter at the antics of the animals caught on home videos. I get teary-eyed when the new baby animals are finally born. (I have to watch the whole show.) I'm amazed at those "top ten extreme" countdowns of animals or insects that can lift 200 times their body weight or do some other absolutely phenomenal feat. Those stories just fascinate me.

I've always loved animals. My dog is my best buddy, my cat provides the entertainment, and my horse takes me on adventures. How many of you have some kind of pet? (*Ask for a show of hands; call out of the various kinds.*)

I love discovering a beautiful view or an unexpected flower or seeing a hawk fly high overhead or a hummingbird flit from blossom to blossom. Father Flanagan of Boys Town said, "Beauty is a silent healer." There is something so refreshing, so peaceful, so cool about nature.

Let's look at a portion of the Creation story from the Bible. (*Read aloud Genesis 1:26-28.*) This passage tells us two important things:

1) God created us in God's own image, and
2) God has given us "dominion" over the rest of creation.

Let's look at the second point first. To "give dominion" is to give power and authority to act. But the word does not say how we are to act in relationship with creation. To know that, we need to know more about being "created in the image of God." What does creation tell us about what God is like?

We look around, and it's pretty clear that God loves beauty. God also must value diversity; just look at the multitude of variations of even one species. Think of a tropical fish tank or a garden, for example, and then multiply that by the thousands upon thousands of species we know. God seems to have a playful streak too. What else can explain a duckbilled platypus or a giraffe?

We are created in the image of this God to love beauty, to value variety, to enjoy creation. God has given us power and authority to act as God's own representatives to care for all of creation. We are to create and preserve beauty, to honor and protect diversity, and to make time and space for enjoying the natural world. What an awesome job! What a privilege!

(*Show the PowerPoint® presentation.*) With scenes such as these, I am filled with awe and gratitude to our Creator God.

But obviously, not everyone has those same feelings. Too many people simply take the natural world for granted. Some people use it and trash it. They "pave paradise to put up a parking lot," as one song says. Others abuse it. Some people are destroyers. Even Animal Planet has stories of horrible animal cruelty. The natural world needs rescuing.

God is calling out the "forest rangers"—you and me. We have a job to do!

Let's pray.

⊙Other Movie Options

Choose this movie, or ask students to recommend a more recent release. Be sure to preview your selection to avoid any content that would be objectionable in your setting. Remember that you must have a video license. (Video licensing information on CD)

• *Bambi* (1942)

Announcements

Dress up volunteers as animals for some purr-fect announcements.

Leader Scripture Exploration

• **Genesis 1** (The first Creation story)
• **Genesis 2:15, 19** (The second Creation story)
• **Psalm 104** (God the Creator and Provider)

⊙On Screen

• Focus Point Enviro-Quiz

• Nature images for Focus Thoughts (PowerPoint® and Text on CD)

• Create a slide show using youth group pictures taken in scenic areas; integrate them into the PowerPoint® scenes that are provided. Or show them as the Focus Point option.

• Connect to *www.myfootprint.org* and project the quiz for the group to take.

⊙Instead of the Message

Read *The Lorax,* by Dr. Seuss (Random House, 1971; ISBN: 034823370). Allow about 10 minutes. Project the pictures on screen if you have the equipment or use the video. (Ordering information on CD)

Create-a-Video Idea

Have members of your group make a commercial encouraging people to recycle.

💿 Service Projects

• Do a quick pick-up. Hand out garbage bags and gloves, and send everyone out for ten minutes only. Ask the group whether they surprised at how much (or how little) trash they found.

• Sponsor a dog wash to raise funds for your local animal shelter.

(Additional ideas on CD)

💿 Out and About

• Go to the zoo. Arrange in advance for a staff person to talk about the zoo's work with endangered species and what the youth can do to support such efforts.

• Take a silent hike. Choose a setting outdoors and have the youth use their eyes to see, ears to hear, fingers to feel, noses to smell, and tongues to taste God's world. Stop at a point along the way to talk about what the youth have experienced. What is God saying to them through nature?

(Additional idea on CD)

Think About It

Treat the earth well. It was not given to you by your parents. It was loaned to you by your children.

—African Proverb

FOCUS GROUP

• What area of caring for God's creation are you already practicing?
• What is another practice that you would like to start?
• Agree or disagree: At a deeper level what needs rescuing is us—from sin, which leads to greed, overuse, consumerism, and demand for convenience at the expense of the natural world.
• What is one thing you've learned in this program that will stay with you?

💿 CLOSING

God's Forest Ranger

Everybody knows that the first person God created was Adam, but dig a little deeper and you'll uncover a lesser-known fact: The word *adam* means "humankind." So when God gives Adam charge of caring for creation, God is putting *us* in charge. Let us dedicate ourselves to the task.

Have the group stand in a circle. Hold a ball of yarn. Tell the group that they will be creating a "web of life." Hold the end of the yarn, name one thing in nature, and toss the ball of yarn to another person in the circle. He or she must do the same, remembering to hold on to the yarn before throwing the ball. Continue until everyone in the circle is included.

Have different persons each make a motion with the web. Observe and feel how everyone is affected because of the connection. Point out that we are all interdependent. What one person does affects others—either positively or negatively.

Ask group members to name human actions that harm the natural world, such as cutting down too many trees or dumping trash or toxic waste. At the mention of each harmful thing, use scissors to cut the web. It will soon start to fall apart.

Then ask for ways to help rescue and care for God's creation. As each suggestion is made, tie the cut pieces together to put the web back again. Close with prayer, reminding the youth that they are called to be God's "forest rangers."

💿 Traditional Native American Prayer (Text on CD)

O Great Spirit,
   whose breath gives life to the world,
   and whose voice is heard in the soft breeze:
We need your strength and wisdom.
Cause us to walk in beauty. Give us eyes
   ever to behold the red and purple sunset.
Make us wise so that we may understand
   what you have taught us.
Help us learn the lessons you have hidden
   in every leaf and rock.
Make us always ready to come to you
   with clean hands and steady eyes,
so when life fades, like the fading sunset,
   our spirits may come to you without shame. Amen.

JUSTICE OF THE PEACE

SOUL FOOD: God calls Christians to rescue people from injustice.

SCRIPTURE: Amos 5:21-24 (God wants justice—not show!)

 ## Games

 ### Move!

Everyone sits in a circle. It your group is very large, form additional circles. The leader calls out a description ("If you have blue eyes . . .") and a number of chairs to skip (". . . move three chairs.") The fun begins when people start stacking up, sitting on someone else's lap, and the bottom person has to move. He or she will need rescuing. (List on CD)

Movin' On Up!

Everyone wants to move up the social ladder, but life just isn't fair. Have the group arrange chairs into a circle and then number off. Use a sticky note or tape to affix the number to the chair. The number belongs to the chair, not the person. As persons move from chair to chair, their number changes. The person whose chair has the highest number is the caller; he or she calls out any number, except the number on his or her chair. The person whose chair has that number has one second (say, "One one hundredths") to call out another number. If a player makes a mistake, he or she goes to the chair with the largest number and becomes the caller. Everyone below the caller moves up a chair. The object of the game is to get to the Number 1 chair.

SHARE AND CARE GROUPS

Checking in: Highs and lows of the week, prayer requests, and prayer

Warm up: How would you define *justice*? How is working for justice different from showing kindness or compassion? Give examples of both.

FOCUS POINT

Video Options: *Remember the Titans* (2000) (Start 59:55; stop 1:02:45). Members of the team, who have forged friendships across racial lines, encounter racism when they try to celebrate together.

Activity Option: What are some things that "squash" people or keep them down in life? Make two lists: one dealing with external factors and one identifying internal factors.

Have It Your Way!

Choose from, adapt, or rearrange these elements to create the best soul feast for your youth group.

THE FIXIN'S

More fun stuff to make the theme extra special! Your choice.

Munchies

- Pizza or pie—but not enough for everyone to have a piece of the pie (unless, of course, the group makes that possible).

- Plain cooked rice, which is what many people survive on

Popular Songs

Use these before and/or after the program to engage the youth. These are some options. Try to include the latest appropriate popular songs.

- "Born in the U.S.A.," by Bruce Springsteen (*Born in the U.S.A.*)
- "(What's So Funny 'Bout) Peace, Love, and Understanding," by Elvis Costello and The Attractions (*The Very Best of Elvis Costello and The Attractions*)
- "Beds Are Burning," by Midnight Oil (*20,000 Watt R.S.L.*)
- "Where Is the Love?" by the Black Eyed Peas (*Elephunk*)
- "The Rose," by Bette Midler (*Greatest Hits—Experience the Divine*)

Worship and Praise Music

- "What Does the Lord Require of You?"
- "Let Justice Roll Down"

 Other Movie Options

Choose this movie, or ask students to recommend a more recent release. Be sure to preview your selection to avoid any content that would be objectionable in your setting. Remember that you must have a video license.
(Video licensing information on CD)

• *Beyond Borders* (R) (2003)

Leader Scripture Exploration

• **Jeremiah 1:4-9** (God calls a young person to speak out for justice.)
• **Amos 5:10-15** (The injustices of Israel)

On Screen

Key points from Focus Thoughts (PowerPoint® and Text on CD)

On-the-Street Interview

Have the youth videotape random youth at the mall (or random church members at various church functions) answering this question: What do you consider to be unjust in our world today?

FOCUS THOUGHTS (Text on CD)

We've been talking about rescuing. We've focused on Jesus as the Chief Firefighter, saving us from the hell of being separated from the love of God. We've heard the call to join God's EMT, to help the hurting people of this world; and we've taken on the challenge to be Forest Rangers, responsible for protecting and rescuing our natural world.

Today we're talking about a not-so-well-known hero. What do you think of immediately when you hear the term the "justice of the peace"? (*Call for the youth to respond.*)

Most people think of the justice of the peace as the one who marries people if they don't get married in a church. Indeed, that is part of the job description. But there is more. The justice of the peace has the authority to act on minor offenses and to commit cases to a higher court for trial. In other words, the justice of the peace rescues people from injustice.

In this theme of Rescue 9-1-1, we've also been talking about God. We've seen that

• God loves the world—you and me, included;
• God loves us so much that God has given Jesus Christ to save us;
• God does not want the world to be condemned;
• God wants good for us—now and always;
• God loves all of us, including the Lazaruses of this world;
• God's vision for the world is not suffering, but healing and wholeness;
• God loves beauty;
• God values diversity;
• God enjoys creation.

But God has another side too. Let's listen to the voice of God through the prophet Amos. (*Read aloud **Amos 5:21-24**.*) We need a bit of context here. God isn't categorically saying, "I hate your worship; I won't accept it." Rather, God is speaking to the people of Israel who, as we would say, had a "Sunday-only faith." The rest of the week was different. According to Amos, the wealthy and powerful trampled on the poor, afflicted the righteous, took bribes, and pushed aside the needy at the gate.

God was calling them—and us—to accountability. If we claim to be Christians, then we need to do more than make a show of worshiping. True worship is in our day-to-day actions. True worship includes rescuing people from injustice. Political and economic systems are used to oppress people and keep them from basic human rights.

"Ah, but," you say, "the injustices of the world are so big; and I am just one small person." Consider the justice of the peace. He or she is not Superman, nor some big-name lawyer or a Justice of the Supreme Court. But the justice of the peace has the authority to act on some offenses and to refer others to a higher court. God calls us to deal with the injustices we can and to turn to the higher court when the offenses are more than we can address.

Most all of us would agree that we want peace. We want people to get along; we don't want war; we want children to grow up without fear. The best way to gain peace is to work for justice.

Let's pray.

FOCUS GROUP

- Give some examples of a "Sunday-only" faith. (No names, please.)
- How does this Scripture add to or take away from your image of God?
- Do love and accountability go together? Why, or why not?
- Racism, sexism, ecological destruction, political oppression, economic oppression, war are areas filled with injustice. Which one of these make you the most angry?
- Anger plus courage lead to hope. What are some actions that you individually or working with friends or as a church can do to work for justice? How might courage be required?
- What are some injustices that you have to refer to a "higher court"? What is the higher court that you refer them to?

CLOSING

God's Justice of the Peace

Speaking out or standing up for justice is not easy. But God calls us to do so. And when God calls us, God gives us the power to do what is necessary. Listen to God's Word. (*Read aloud **Jeremiah 1:4-9.***)

Do not say, "I am only a teenager." You are called by God; God has known you and loved since before you were born. God will be with you. Work for justice. Work for peace. Amen.

Make Me an Instrument of Peace (Handout on CD)

The Prayer of Saint Francis of Assisi captures the essence of this program. Give the youth a copy of the prayer. Pray it in unison or with two groups alternating lines.

The prayer has also been set to music "Make Me a Channel of Peace."

Out and About

- Take the youth to a courtroom to witness a trial.
- Plan for an eye-opening trip. Have the group attend a seminar on a social injustice. (Information on CD)

Service Projects

- Write letters to elected representatives about dealing with issues such as poverty and hunger at the institutional level. (List of addresses on CD)
- Write letters on behalf of Amnesty International, an organization that works for human rights. (Information on CD)
- Do an Empty Bowls event to fight against hunger. High school students started this program! (Information on CD)

Go Deeper

Commit to a six-week study about haves and have nots. (Information on CD)

Witness Statement

Invite a youth or an adult to talk about his or her experience working for justice. (How-to on CD)

Bumper Stickers

If you want peace, work for justice.

No justice, no peace.
Know justice. Know peace.

COMBOS CD-ROM

Starting the Program

PC/Windows®
The CD-Rom is designed to automatically start when you insert it into your PC. If it does not start automatically, you will need to run the Combos application.

Bring up your directory listing (on Microsoft®, use Explore or My Computer). You will see one subdirectory, "combos," and two files, "autorun" and "Combos." Double-click on the Combos application.

Macintosh®
Double-click on the CD-Rom icon. A pop-up window will appear with OS9 or OSX as options. Double-click on the icon that matches your computer's operating system.

If you get an error message that says, "Could not find the application program ...," choose your browser application (for example, Internet Explorer, Netscape, Safari). Once you have done this, you should not have the error message upon opening the CD-Rom in the future.

You can access the subdirectory in the folder named "combos" before you choose your operating system or by clicking on an item such as a presentation or a poster.

Handouts, Presentations, Logos, Posters, Talks

Handouts and some of the other files on the CD-Rom are saved in Adobe Acrobat® (pdf files). To open them, you will need the Adobe Acrobat® Reader installed on your computer. If you do not have Adobe Acrobat® Reader, log on to the Internet while running the CD; click on the Adobe Acrobat® Reader link at the bottom of any page. This will take you to the page where you can download the free reader from Adobe.

On a Macintosh: If you click on a pdf link and receive an error message labeled "Unhandled File Type," choose "Application" and then find the Adobe Acrobat® application on your hard drive.

Presentations that say "PowerPoint®" will launch in your PC browser window. If you have Microsoft® PowerPoint® on your computer and wish to save or modify the presentations, you can click Save As and save them to your hard drive. (On a Macintosh, a

directory of PowerPoint® presentations will open. The presentation file that you clicked on is highlighted. Double-click the file to open it, or click and hold your mouse and drag the file to your desktop if you want to save or modify the presentation.)

To get editable text from the **Talks** is to highlight the text from the Focus Thoughts version that you want and copy it, then paste it into your word processing program.

If you want to save any of the files—handouts, presentations, logos, posters—to your hard drive, you can also go to the Combos sub-directory (on Microsoft®, use Explore or My Computer). **Posters** and **theme_logos** have their own sub-directory under the Combos sub-directory. PowerPoint® presentations can be found in the sub-directory for the theme. For instance, if you want the PowerPoint® presentation for the Awesome Power of Perseverance, click on the 05_AWESOME sub-directory; then click on the 02_perseverance.ppt file.

Minimum System Requirements

PC/Windows®
Pentium® II 300 MHz or faster processor
Microsoft® Windows 98 or later
64 MB RAM
4X CD-ROM Drive
Internet Explorer 5.0 or Higher Recommended
QuickTime® 5.0 or higher
External speakers recommended

Macintosh®
PowerPC 300 MHZ or faster processor
Mac OS 9.0 or later
64 MB RAM
4X CD-ROM Drive
Internet Explorer 5.0 or Higher Recommended for OS9
Safari or Internet Explorer Recommended for OS X
QuickTime® 5.0 or higher

Abingdon Technical Support

If you have difficulty launching the program, you may call Abingdon technical support at 615-749-6777, Monday through Friday, 8 a.m. to 5 p.m., Central Standard Time.